The Ego

The Body and Beyond

Yagesh Nohwal

Made with ♥ on the Notion Press Platform

www.notionpress.com

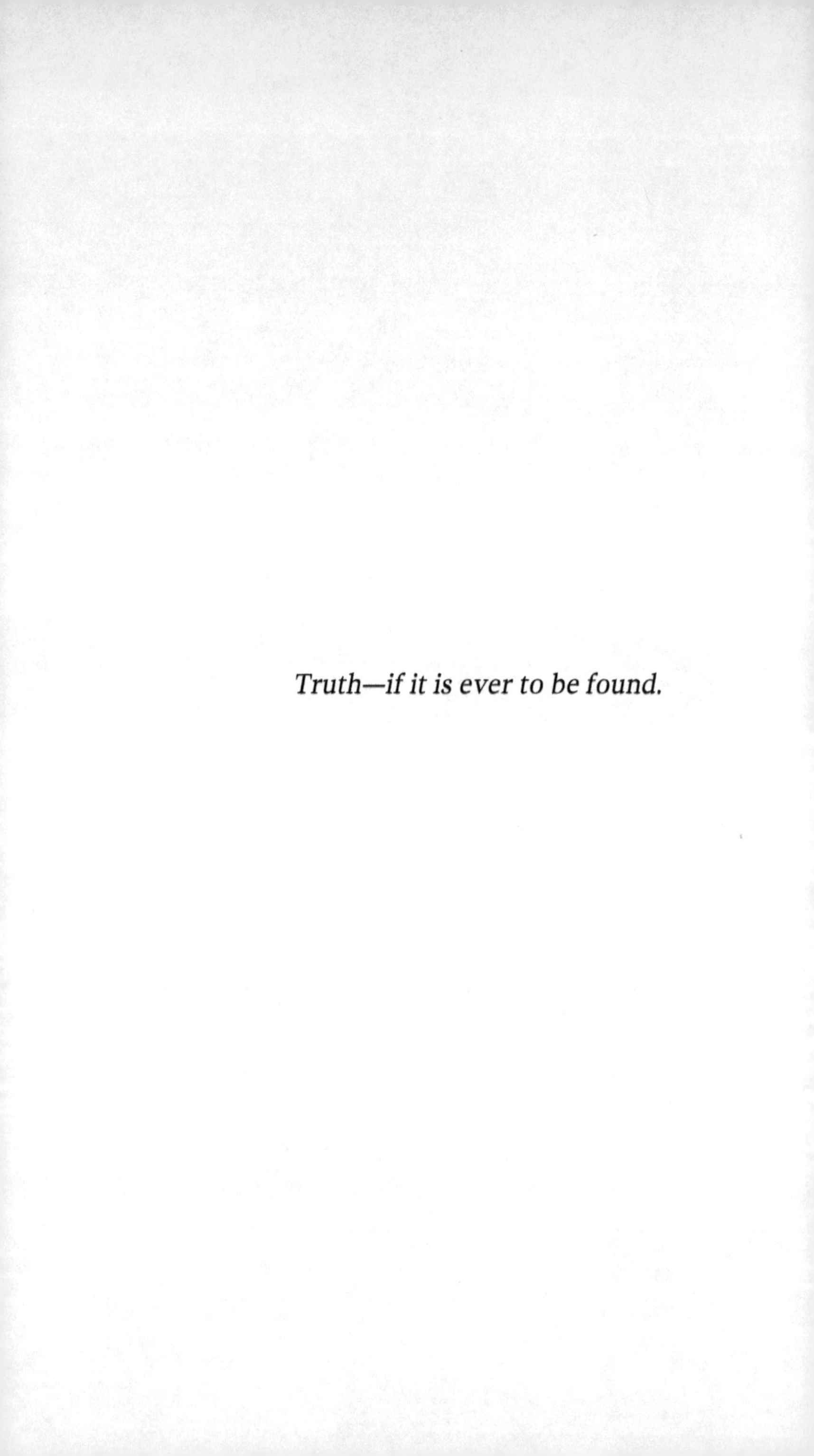

Truth—if it is ever to be found.

Contents

CONTENTS

Preface

This work was born from a series of insights into the psychic faculty called the "ego." The trail of insights hit me while reading *The Uncanny* by Sigmund Freud. Whether that be the corporeality of the ego, its inseparable relation to bodily parts like the skin, or its dependence on touch for maintaining cohesion, it all appeared to me through insights whose origin was non-intellectual; it was only later that through my formal education and course material, I could verify their validity.

Though this work was initially intended to be published solely as my Master's dissertation at Ambedkar University, Delhi; I did not want my ideas to be forgotten and collect dust in the university library. November of 2023 marked the beginning of a series of dissatisfactions in me regarding the process of writing the dissertation. My supervisor was quick to dismiss my idea that there could be something more to the script of the ego than the body. His arguments—backed by popular scientific "facts"—revolved around the 'aim' of existence being survival and reproduction. I heard somewhere of a Buddhist teaching that says, "In moments of hunger, giving away your food will make you stronger." It is the truth in teachings like these which go beyond popular science, that prevented me from dismissing the essence of life as survival and copulation. I am grateful to a couple of my professors from whom I received positive feedback in regard to my ideas around concepts like *The Eye Ego* and the psychic importance of the shadow. Multiple of these ideas could not make it into the dissertation, for which I have decided to publish them myself.

This work has emerged in the absence of any clinical experience but very much in the presence of life experiences. I like to believe that I am sensitive enough to catch subtle experiences both in myself and in the people around me; it is from those observations that I have been able to build this system of thought. If, in the future, I find evidence that suggests something against the validity of my claims, I hope I do not shy away from abandoning these ideas without much hesitation, as it is truth alone that I am in search of. Spending time with one's thoughts, especially if they are the of kind that can earn you recognition and appraisal, tempts you to hold on to them tightly. I hope this does not happen to me, as my loyalty is to the truth—if it is ever to be found in these advanced versions of addition and subtraction. I hope my work lives up to the expectations of the reader.

Yagesh Nohwal

16th September 2024

Prologue

This work aims to study the dynamics of the ego from various perspectives, using tools such as psychoanalysis, phenomenology, and meditation. Drawing on knowledge from diverse disciplines—including biopsychology, social and cultural symbols, developmental theories, autobiographical accounts, and popular literature—this book does not merely restate or revise existing knowledge. Instead, it situates my claims as credible through their sensibility and support from recognized theories. By engaging with multiple sources, this work presents a multifaceted understanding of the ego. Each perspective brings something unique to the discussion. Yet, as with any discourse on the ego, this work cannot encompass the full breadth of such a vast and intricate concept. I have found compelling evidence about various aspects of the ego and I am sharing these findings with you, acknowledging that none of them are absolute or beyond debate. They remain open to reconstruction, deconstruction, approval, or disapproval— just like any other psychological concept.

A classical view of the ego's genesis suggests that it originates from the id, primarily to manage the reality principle, which conflicts with the pleasure principle—the mode of operation of the id. As infants experience pain and frustration when their desires are unmet, there arises a need for a system to help discharge impulses and achieve gratification in ways that align with reality. The emergence of the 'self' is simultaneous with the development of the ego and is entirely dependent on it. The body, as the host of sensations and the container of the 'I', becomes the foundational point for the development of the ego. Freud referred to this as the "body-ego": the core from which the ego begins to develop and expand. The body—more specifically, the senses—becomes the source of sensations that contribute to the birth of the ego. While this simplified explanation serves as an introduction to the concept, it is important to note that my claims about the body ego go beyond sensations alone. For example, body hair may not produce sensations, but it plays a crucial role in our sense of identity, intimacies, and mental well-being.

The functions of the ego are vast, ranging from organizing experiences into a coherent narrative that fits within the broader life story to making sense of experiences, containing unconscious forces, and finding realistic ways to gratify one's needs. Early psychoanalysts believed these needs to be purely biological. The ego also plays a crucial role in mediating between two realities—internal and external. Significant contributions in the field have been made by thinkers such as Donald Winnicott, Carl Jung, Jacques Lacan, and Didier Anzieu. At this point, it is essential to grasp the basic understanding that the ego is a psychic entity tasked with maintaining peace between conflicting parts of the mind. Without the ego, a person—or any organism—would be driven entirely by internal forces (drives) and external circumstances, lacking any agency of their own.

Meaning-making, empathy, and social and personal identity are all products of the ego.

As this book explores the dynamics of the ego in the present moment, it is important to acknowledge the mechanisms the ego uses to protect itself from threats to its integrity. Ego defenses play a crucial role in maintaining the structure of the psyche throughout life, and a significant amount of energy is spent on functions such as repression, introjection, denial, projection, splitting, and reaction formation. However, defense is a secondary function of the ego. The primary function, as I see it, is to maintain its current shape and execute its duties efficiently. Only afterward does it focus on self-protection from internal and external forces. The ego, as a living entity, is responsible not only for protecting the organism from distress but also for maintaining its integrity. This "maintenance of integrity" is a function of the ego. I may interchangeably refer to these as "features" or "characteristics," depending on the context, as I find these terms synonymous in relation to the ego (in some contexts).

When we consider the ego as a concept in academic psychology, we find neither a single, definitive explanation nor consensus around its nature and functions. Even within psychoanalysis, the idea of the ego is contested, with different schools offering divergent views on "what the ego is". Despite its importance as a psychic entity, the complexity of the ego often goes unrecognized and underappreciated. Existing discourse is not only scattered but also filled with conflicting perspectives, making it challenging to develop a unified understanding of it. The literature rarely provides a comprehensive or multifaceted view of the concept. Instead, the ego is frequently addressed selectively or fragmentarily, often in support of other psychological constructs or to strengthen arguments within particular contexts. In other words, the ego is treated as a secondary concern, with its exploration serving other primary topics of interest.

Moreover, centralized resources offering a holistic understanding of the ego are scarce. Most available literature engages with the concept only peripherally, and those that do address it directly often take a narrow approach, dedicated to specific schools of thought. This work seeks to resolve both of these issues by presenting a comprehensive study of the dynamic nature of the ego, drawing on theories and observations from a wide array of disciplines. Traditionally, clinical researchers focus on the ego through their observations of pathological states, often overlooking cultural symbols and broader literature. In this book, I aim to fill that gap, addressing what I perceive to be a significant shortcoming in existing literature.

Section A: I

Chapter One
Conscious Ego

If introspection were a valid research tool, it would confine the study of the ego to the conscious plain. Nonetheless, it would personally and academically be a satiating pursuit. Beginning with introspection, it is natural for anyone to conclude the "I" as an observer of the experiences. The watcher of the world, the smeller of the odors, and the listener of the voices (pun intended). Apart from being the witness of the spatio-temporal world, the "I" also acts as the anchor or a reference point for thoughts and a point of orientation for the person to navigate life. If this endeavour of inspecting the ego through introspection—consciousness—could be taken by the tools of Phenomenology, it would crudely reduce the ego as the point of referral—the "I", which is much less wealthy than the psychoanalytic ego. However, the benefit would be in the freshness of the method. Psychoanalysis, with its orientation, tends to totally neglect the conscious 'I', leaving phenomenology with an opportunity to do it. Phenomenological principles tell us that if the 'world' was to not be attributed with personal meanings, the ego, for certain, would temporarily cease to be a resident of the consciousness. By this statement, Phenomenology indicates the plausible nature of the "I"—that it exists only in active relation to experiences.

It would not be wrong to state that every thinker who sets on to think about the general human condition or about the 'self' eventually discovers that within the mind, there is a faculty that positions the human in the world and acts as an anchor. Recognition of a 'psychic faculty' that has specific characteristics and tendencies and which has been talked about by thinkers and religions from different time periods in history is evidence in itself of the existence of such a faculty. One fine demonstration of collective human intelligence is the acknowledgment of the "ego". A social adoption of the "ego" and making it a part of the everyday vocabulary suggests to me that the knowledge of "ego" as a psychic feature serves a purpose for us humans. By this, I mean that having knowledge of such a feature serves a purpose even for the common folks. It would only be a speculation, but the use of this socially acknowledged term helps people to have a formal opinion about their identity; "it is my ego that makes me be the way I am". This tells that the ego also has a need for constant assurance of its existence. One of the contents of consciousness is its own knowledge.

Phenomenology

A formal academic view of the ego that uses introspection as its tool of choice to understand the ego in a manner that is beyond auto-biographical in its accounts, and seeks to find the universal nature of the ego is Phenomenology. The classic Phenomenological belief is that consciousness is always 'of' something, as it exists in an active relation to its content. Wherever there is a content of consciousness, there has to be a subject, to which these momentary contents of consciousness have to be subjected; this was called the "Pure ego" by Husserl.[1] When there is awareness of content—there is experience—there has to be 'something' that is experiencing—the "I"—the empirical ego. This suggests that phenomenology acknowledges the existence of a subjective entity that acts as the reference point for the experiences so they can be woven into a cohesive harmony, the reference point to which is always the "I". Husserlian "*epoche*" poses here as a challenge to the above-established fact that there is always an "I" that becomes a witness to the world. Husserlian *epoche* asks the observer to suspend the world objects of their subjective status and associations, so the "I"—the empirical ego has no function to serve and, therefore, disappears; what then is left is the "Pure ego". Knowledge of this Pure ego opens up a new layer of the ego: that there is more to the conscious ego than the "I".

This leaves us with two possible characteristics of the ego:

- The content of the consciousness is associated with the "I", so a cohesive, meaningful relation with the world is established.

- This "I" can be suspended at will

Referring to the mental apparatus introduced by Freud in his remarkable work "*The Interpretation of Dreams*"[2], we can learn where this conscious "I" resides and what might be its genesis or mechanism. Phenomenology is concerned with the "sensible" end of the apparatus; here we get an opportunity to learn about a single layer of the ego. For a long time, it has been an opinion in philosophy, and specifically in Jungian psychology, that the ego is at the centre of our consciousness, and all the experiences are referred to what we know as the "I"—which is a resident of consciousness.[3] If we attempt to situate this "I" (the empirical ego) on Freud's psychic apparatus, it would have to be placed immediately behind the sensible end, with an ability to communicate with the deeper layers of the system. This communication happens bi-directionally, with it being able to recall memories for its sustenance at the moment, and also being able to position the experiences into the memory system with its own omissions and associations. Though memories can be formed during the absence of the empirical ego, solely thanks to the Pure ego. "The pure ego is a phenomenological residuum of the *epoche*".[4] But the "I" has an active influence over the memory disposition and experience sense-making; this might even be one of the reasons for the sustenance of core-beliefs and existing psychic autobiography (how people see themselves in the grand scheme of things and life narratives, it is one of the recognised reasons for psychological distress according to multiple therapeutic models). An anecdotal demonstration of the *'epoche'* or any Eastern meditations can be used to prove the above-mentioned claim. During meditative states, a person usually claims to have lost a sense of self and practically achieves the state that phenomenologists call the "*epoche*". Here, the person may still register sensory inputs and memories but does not form any evaluative relations with them. These memories, when recalled in future, still retain the subjective perspective as a result of a particular position held by the person in the spatiotemporal world, but not necessarily any personal associations or emotional charges. These memories are registered in the absence of the "I"; therefore, the "I" couldn't effectively arrange them into different memory systems as a result of not being able to form an associative relation with them and pre-formed memories. So, if the speculation is correct, people's experiences and relations with the memories formed during meditations—an *epoche*—would confirm this. This claim of mine that experiences that are gained in the absence of the *"I"*, essentially lack a personal narrative is complemented by philosophies like Buddhism and Stoicism; where Buddhism, with its concept of Satipatthana (bare attention), asks the practitioner to be disidentified with their awareness, results in the observation of the experiences as insignificant occurrences in consciousness.[5] Similar is a Stoic practice by Marcus Aurelius, called "view from the above".[6] Both of these practices have been scientifically shown to reduce personal and emotional engagement with experiences in studies by Brefczynski[7] and Learmonth et al. (2015), respectively. I claim this happens due to the absence of the "I", that is responsible for knitting experiences in a singular grand narrative—the life story. Here, we learn that the ego, as a dynamic entity, has a provision to modulate its shape and functions if necessary by not letting 'subjectivity' overtake the purity of an experience. Evidence for the claim will be provided once I firmly establish the direction and the tools that I am choosing to investigate the features of the conscious ego.

Hyle and *Noetic* Phase

Before we move ahead to talk about features of the ego, it would benefit us to talk about the phenomenological phases called *"Hyle"* and *"Noetic"*. *Hyle* means the 'material', which does not necessarily have a meaning in itself, and when consciousness acknowledges it without making any sense of it, it's called the *"hyle"* phase. *Noesis* or the noetic phase then animates these meaningless sensory experiences with 'appropriate' meaning. It is exactly the job of the Pure ego to see a potential field of experiences and seek to paint them in a specific colour.

Putting this in perspective of the psychic apparatus and the characteristics of the "empirical" and the "pure" ego, we learn that the ever-present communication between the conscious and the unconscious is not something to be taken for granted. The independence of these two phases and the reliance of the more critical phase on the Pure ego, i.e. noesis, tells us that we humans have the ability to see the world in an uncontaminated form, which perhaps indicates a possibility that the ego has the quality to retreat back to the Pcs and the Ucs, leaving behind the Cs. This assumption shall be stretched to its limits further in the text.

Clarity on this "retreat" would be achieved by recalling the Freudian psychic apparatus, as it proposes the sensible end to have a quality to contain the sensory experiences without actually having any long-lasting impressions of those experiences; in his text *Mystic Writing-Pad*,[8] he compares the perception-memory relation to a thin sheet placed on a wax layer, which due to its materialistic characteristic retains nothing that is scribbled on it. The hyle phase is a philosophical interpretation of the same phenomenon, which demonstrates that the ego, despite allegedly being the core of consciousness, leaves scope for the objects to not be contaminated by the "I"—the empirical ego. I presume that for a prolonged hyle phase to occur, the connection between the conscious and the other fractions of the mind, i.e. the pre-conscious and the unconscious (the expressway for which might be the *ego)*, must be cut off for an amount of time. The initiation of this disconnection happens primarily by a halt in the communication between different fractions of the mind. This leaves us with two considerations:

- The ego, as a dynamic force, has the ability to step back from the consciousness and revert back to its point of origin, deeper in the mind.

- The supply of the psychic energy (libido), needed for the functioning of different fractions of the mind (Cs, Pcs and Ucs), undergoes a dynamic shift.

These speculations may seem to be distant, but are actually complimentary to each other. Perhaps a great wealth of knowledge awaits us if we study both of these potential facts independently.

Egolessness

The idea of the ego not existing seems to be an unlikely one, and that is for all the right reasons; what is being proposed is not a cessation of the ego from the psyche, but its absence from the consciousness—with all its defences, affects, thoughts, intentions and most importantly the 'I'. In the ordinary state, the ego, in order to ensure its sustenance 'at the moment', engages with a stream of autobiographical thoughts, familiar affective states, memories and revised ideas. It, at all times, is engaged with the production and self-consumption of a script that nurtures its sustenance. On top of this, the newly gained experiences are also labelled with "I", "my", or "mine", making them relate to the ego; the ego appropriates them to itself.

The ego is primarily born out of the Id, to let the Id survive with its irrationality amid the presence of the realities of the world, and for this, the ego serves as a buffer between the external world and the Id. The ego is at all times involved in momentary calculations and adjustments to ensure the organism's well-being, which, in absolute terms, depends on its own cohesiveness. Its purpose is to rescue the person from unbearable anxieties and intolerable experiences. I suggest that if an 'appropriate' environment is provided for the person, *the ego would halt its functions and cease to be*—until the "appropriateness" of the environment is maintained. As this chapter is solely concerned with the conscious ego, the phenomenological perspective is my first chronological choice to understand the ego, followed by meditation.

Here, first-person experiences of mental states—where the essential functions of the conscious ego, the *"I"*, *memory associations, bodily movements and awareness*, and the ability to establish *communication* are to be observed during a state of meditation. The rationale behind my choice to observe these aspects of the psyche is to study the validity of my claim that "there indeed can be a disappearance of the conscious ego". I see these functions to be in close association with the conscious ego, and any modulations in them would provide us with relevant information about the state of the ego. The reason behind choosing meditation to study this claim is that it is traditionally believed to cause a dissolution of the ego, and its mechanism resonates with the phenomenological techniques of not engaging with the world at will. I think it would be of benefit for us to remember that the purpose of studying the ego during meditative phases is not to study the effects of meditation but to study the properties of the ego in these highly specialised conditions. I call 'meditation' a specialised condition because here, a person can employ their *will* to create unordinary psychic conditions—where the person is in a state of meta-awareness, while also maintaining the absence of the self-image cathexis.

Meditation

Meditative practices all over the world begin with asking the practitioner to make modulations in their body posture, immediate environment and sensory stimulations before initiating the practice—with the assumption that this would make the person experience changes in their thoughts, affects, and the idea of the *self*. It is worth noticing that the *body*, the *environment*, the affects (both conscious and unconscious), and the "I" are either the productions or the attending sites for the ego. The meeting point of the body, the environment and the internal state, quintessentially, is the site where the ego has its greatest job to perform. By this, I mean that the genesis of the ego happens to handle the environment and the *Id*, to help the person navigate their world with relative ease and minimum dysfunction. The ego recognises the body as its vehicle and navigates the world likewise. If 'appropriate' conditions are curated, with the modulations in the environment, the ego can perhaps retire for a time, and a cease would occur in its functions. This "cease" is an unordinary psychic event resulting from unordinary environmental arrangements. In this "practice", the body is positioned in a specific posture known as आसन

(*āsana*), which is to be maintained without disturbance for extended durations. The sensory organs are recommended to undergo deprivation of stimulation, and the individual is instructed not to engage with any stimuli that manage to penetrate—a prolonged hyle phase. This state can be perceived as the absence of the external 'world' and the non-requirement of bodily engagement. Consequently, the dual sources of demand for the ego—the corporeal and environmental (experienced through the senses)—fade away, providing the ego an opportunity to retreat. And if this "fade" is real, we would also trace it in certain psychic functions and experiences, namely *Communication, Psychosis* and the *"I"*. By Communication, I refer to the capacity to articulate coherent sentences to convey one's internal cognitive states to others and engage in internal self-dialogue, which necessitates having a grasp of linguistic structures such as syntax and semantics. This linguistic proficiency is not merely confined to conscious awareness; rather, it resides within the deeper recesses of the mind. However, without a robust conscious ego, the individual's adeptness in constructing sentences through skilful language employment, which inherently relies on the dynamic interplay between conscious and pre-conscious mental faculties, becomes compromised and essentially non-existent.

"Meditation is the dissolution of thoughts in eternal awareness or pure consciousness without objectification, knowing without thinking, merging finitude in infinity."   ~Swami Sivananda

A state of effortless 'living' is achieved when a person is able to accomplish a thoughtless state by employing their 'will'. According to Carl Jung, the supposed *"free will"*, too, just like any other mental feature, is a form of energy' or more appropriately "a representative of the libido".[9] Here it should be said that Jung did not believe the person to have an absolute will of their own, but is under unconscious forces. Here, I speculate that a plausible explanation can be that there is an unconscious wish for ego dissolution and possibly attain an egoless state or even a higher goal of मुक्ति—that derives one to abandon the known plains of consciousness during meditation.

Typically, a person's experience of the meditation begins by setting themselves in a posture that does not demand readjustments (these "readjustments" would come from any discomforts that cause the mind to attend to the body); hence, any demands of the body are prevented by keeping it stationed in a motionless revised position. The next step typically involves closing the eyes (arguably one of the most important sensory organs, alongside the *skin*). The practitioner also begins not to attend if there are any noises in the environment, and with this, all the sense organs (gateways of the external world) are effectively cut out. Now the situation is such that the external world and the *body—ego's* functions have been taken care of—by effectively preventing any circumstances that would call for their services. Though the biological clock would eventually bring the mind back to bodily requirements, till then, the mind can afford to be negligent of the body. After the world has disappeared, thoughts and emotions take over the attention, which would be met by the same reaction from the practitioner, by the use of 'will'. A state of effortless 'living' is achieved when a person is able to accomplish a thoughtless state by employing their 'will', which is accompanied by self-image decathexis.

The 'will', which I refer to here, is the representative of the individual's supposed autonomy over their mind. The 'will', as a faculty that directs and redirects libido, is used to cause dynamic shifts in one's psychic states during meditation. This willful neglect of the world around oneself and withdrawal of senses facilitates greater sensitivity towards one's internal state.

Now let me explain what is so particular about meditation, for a greater clarity on what is about to follow. Meditation needs the person to rest the body in a set posture, with an active negation of the senses. The primary reason for the genesis of the ego is to serve the body and its relations to the environment. Hence the 'body' and the 'external world' are sites that demand the ego's service. Now that they have been "taken care of", the ego retires from these responsibilities till the time this condition of worldly withdrawal and bodily rest persists.

Now that I have claimed that the ego has been given the opportunity to rest, let's observe the validity of my claim. If the conscious ego is indeed absent, then it should undoubtedly be traceable in its functions, and for that, I am choosing the aspect of **communication** and **time perception**[10]—as both of these are functions of the ego. A halt or malfunction in both of these functions would prove that the ego is incapable of performing its duties—as it is absent—in states of meditation. Apart from the absence of these two mental functions that occur at the cusp of the self and the world—the body, the ego is also responsible for protecting the consciousness from the unconscious content. The internal job of the ego is to work as a censoring faculty that keeps undesired material repressed by guarding the gates of consciousness, and if the conscious ego is truly absent, we shall find evidence of the unconscious leaking into the conscious.

References

1. Husserl, Edmund, Ideas: A General Introduction to Pure Phenomenon. Translated by W. R. Boyce Gibson. New York: Humanities Press INC., 1969
2. Freud, S. (1900). *The Interpretation of Dreams*. Macmillan.
3. Jung, C. G. (1960). *The Structure and Dynamics of the Psyche*. Princeton University Press.
4. Husserl: §57, p. 173 and §80, p. 233
5. Gethin, R. (2001). *The Foundations of Buddhism*. Oxford University Press
6. Robertson, D. (2019). *How to Think Like a Roman Emperor: The Stoic Philosophy of Marcus Aurelius*. St. Martin's Press.
7. Brefczynski-Lewis, J. A., Lutz, A., Schaefer, H. S., Levinson, D. B., & Davidson, R. J. (2007).
8. Freud, S. (1925). *A note upon the 'Mystic Writing Pad'*. In J. Strachey (Ed. & Trans.), The Standard Edition of the Complete Psychological Works of Sigmund Freud (Vol. 19, pp. 227-232). Hogarth Press
9. Jung, C. G. (1960). *The Structure and Dynamics of the Psyche* (R. F. C. Hull, Trans.). Princeton University Press.
10. *Fliess, R. (1961). Ego and Body Ego: Contributions to Their Psychoanalytic Psychology. International Universities Press*

Chapter Two

Ego Dissolution

A Leak

A recurring theme has been observed in my collected accounts. Practitioners with whom I enquired, have reported experiencing vivid mental imagery resembling dreams even while being awake, which unequivocally signals the absence of the conscious ego—traced through the ineffectiveness of its defence mechanisms. I posit that the mind, with its various facets, operates dynamically at all times. However, it is the ego's role to ensure that these facets remain in balance, thereby averting any potential flood of conflicting elements and consequent pathological dysfunction. An omnipresent function of the mind, specifically the unconscious, is to dream. The unconscious mind is in a perpetual state of activity, consistently fulfilling its functions, among which is the process of dreaming. Nevertheless, fortified by its defences against disruptive and intolerable content, the conscious ego serves as a barrier, preventing dreams from infiltrating conscious awareness. It is when the conscious ego is subdued during meditation that these defensive barriers become ineffective, allowing dreams to emerge into consciousness.

For my dissertation, I interviewed a young meditation practitioner named Mohit. In one of his meditation accounts, he reports having experienced an unusual occurrence, which "nobody would believe". One day, while meditating on a metro ride, having closed his eyes, he fell into a dream-like state. He dreamt of seeing a man in a grey shirt standing at a distance from him. After some time, as he opened his eyes, he reports, "I saw the same man in a grey shirt standing right where I had imagined him to be". While there could be any number of interpretations of this experience of his, there is only one condition for which it occurred. It must be mentioned that I am not vouching for any supernatural experiences that supposedly arise during meditation; instead, I look at this account as purely a (mildly) psychotic one. The person feels no hesitation in mentioning their irrational experience, which tells that there must have been a malfunction in the faculty of reality testing. There can be two possibilities for this experience of theirs. **First:** he caught a glimpse of the person wearing the grey shirt before closing his eyes, and later mistook the memory for a spiritual experience. **Second:** he saw the person for the first time after opening his eyes, and only later, in retrospect, the image of the person was added into the memory system. In both cases, the only possibility is that Mohit was in a state of weakened ego, which enabled such a fault in his memory system.

At this point, I would like to refer to an autobiographical account[*][†] to supplement and

---

* *The personal reason that motivated me to explore this idea comes from my own experience of witnessing mild hallucinations as a result of practising 'dhyan' after reading Swami Vivekanand's Raj-Yog. Not particularly during the meditative state, but anytime throughout the day, I would see human-like figures in my peripheral vision, which would last not more than a second. These were low-resolution shadow-like figures that did not have any unique characteristics to them. Upon discussing with other people, I learnt that this is a relatively common phenomenon among people who practice this style of meditation. Some people also stated that they would hear monotonous sounds throughout the day, and they did not know if this experience was unique to them. Swami Vivekanand, in his Raja Yoga, states that practising yoga brings many experiences to the practitioner that would otherwise be considered impossible. Smelling things that are not in a person's immediate environment, hearing people talk from a far-away distance, or knowing other's thoughts are some of the experiences that people have as a result of his prescribed practices.[2] Now that I have inspected it in retrospect, I find that the cause of these experiences must have been a weakened ego that could not contain the unconscious. I do not aim to analyse the psychotic experiences that I just mentioned, as that would not serve the topic of the dissertation, but a reference to them hopefully contributes to the running discourse of ego dissolution.*
Apart from these hallucinations, I also stumbled upon another realization. It was during one of those meditation sessions that I experienced a peculiar phenomenon—I entered a dream state while being fully awake. This occurrence began to manifest randomly thereafter, leading me to the realization that my mind is at all times immersed in dreams, regardless of whether I am asleep or not. It dawned on me that dreaming is a natural state for the unconscious, and it is the ego that prevents us

enhance the ongoing discourse. It is entirely up to the reader if they take my words for what they are. It was this realization that serves as the foundation for this section of the book, and a tolerance for the idea of the possibility that ego can indeed dissolve.

While mine is a personal account, there are published records of people who have had experiences of psychosis that were triggered specifically by their meditative practices. Adyashanti's memoir "The End of Your World"[2], records the psychotic episodes that came after her rigorous meditation. She mentions that she spent around 4 years in an altered state of consciousness, where she could not even recognise herself in the mirror. I am refraining from engaging in the nature of their psychosis, as my purpose here is to demonstrate that the ego is indeed absent during meditation, the effects of which are seen in the form of failed defences against the unconscious content.

---

† from slipping into this abyss. Dreams do not 'occur' in a dungeon, but they have the ability to influence our consciousness. A dream is like a magnet that arranges ferromagnetic metals according to its magnetic flow. It occurred to me—without any forceful thinking—that I have always been under the influence of these omnipresent dreams and the parallel unconscious life. My unconscious life arranges the environmental occurrences in my realization. It is as if my life is navigated by my conscious contents being arranged in a rhythm that originates unconsciously. The design of my consciousness is a product of the unconscious and not just a matter of chance that could be taken for granted.

Communication

Speech is essentially absent in states of meditation, as speech is a function that is not passive as merely "seeing" something but relies on access to the pre-conscious memory systems—for an appropriate vocabulary to be retrieved, to be able to assess the listener's responses and make modulations, and finally to comprehend the incoming information and make sense of it. Since the ego is absent, the two-way communication between the "I" and the memory systems is compromised. Hence, language—that is stored in the memory systems cannot be accessed. Communication requires making sense of the incoming stimulation, comprehending it based on one's knowledge registered in the memory, and then choosing the proper responses. Not being able to speak out loud, is what is expected from a person engaging in meditation. It may seem unimpressive to pay attention to the inability to speak, but it is anything but insignificant. Cease in communication may seem obvious when the person is reserved in their own self, withdrawn from the world, and willingly unengaged with thoughts, but this 'cease' is not consequential; instead, it is circumstantial. This means that the person does not engage in communication out of unimportance of communication during moments of meditation, but they are in an internal state that does not provide the facility of sentence construction. The "cease" that I talk about here is not a total annihilation of the ability of different systems to interact with each other, but of the purposeful 'digging-out', that is a feature of the ordinary "I"; as the "I" being the representative of the supposed *'free-will'*. The "I" is what is the commanding force of intention (of sentence construction in this case). As a writer, I have been unable to find or produce any firsthand accounts of individuals' experiences of failing to communicate or form coherent sentences during meditation. This is likely because such an experience would be highly subjective and challenging (for those affected) to articulate or make sense of. Furthermore, there appears to be no research or scholarly sources explicitly exploring this specific phenomenon. Therefore, the validity of this claim about impaired communication and language production primarily rests on the resonance it finds within the reader's own experiences and personal observations.

Time Perception

Subjective differences in time perception have been a concern for Psychology, Philosophy and Physics. With the introduction of Psychoanalysis, 'time perception' has been seen as a conscious experience, as the unconscious is "timeless". The creation of the ego is the beginning of binding experiences in a temporal cohesion.[3] Experience of time is affected by affective states like *boredom, impatience, happiness, sleep* and *dreams;* which demonstrates that time perception is *subjective.* Engaging with the mechanism of time perception is not our goal here, but to observe if time perception is indeed affected under meditation; if so, it would be evidence of the ego being absent from consciousness.

Convincing the reader of the validity of my claim should not be a very difficult task, as asking any meditation practitioner about their perception of time is bound to garner expected answers, as this is a widely acknowledged phenomenon for meditators to experience a 'break' in their sense of time as if they were in a state of sleep. There are some cases of experiencing 'boredom', which arises if the person is not able to achieve a meditative state and is left bored due to lack of sensory stimulation. I got to know from a Yoga instructor about the commonality of people experiencing a loss in time perception, "as if they had fallen into a different world, detached from the body and chatter of the mind". A similar account by N.S. Hirman, is found on a Yoga foundation's web portal.[4] Freud explained the perception of time as an experience arising from the oscillation of cathexis between sensory experiences and the perceptive aspect of the conscious (Pcpt-Cs). Meditation eliminates this cathexis oscillation that is tracked by the ego, hence proving that the ego is indeed absent during meditation.

*

References

1. Adyashanti. (2009). *The End of Your World: Uncensored Straight Talk on the Nature of Enlightenment.* Sounds True.

2. Vivekananda, S. (1896). *Raja Yoga.* Ramakrishna-Vivekananda Center

3. Fliess, R. (1961). *Ego and Body Ego: Contributions to Their Psychoanalytic Psychology* (p. 182). International Universities Press.

4. Ananda. (n.d.). *Going in and out of consciousness during meditation.* Ananda. Retrieved September 4, 2024, from https://www.ananda.org/ask/going-in-and-out-of-consciousness-during-meditation/

Chapter Three

Libidinal investment into the 'I'

In this section, I shall explore the second consideration: *the ego in need of libidinal supply.* We reached this possibility by deducing that the ego goes through a dynamic shift under certain circumstances, and as a result, it halts some of its functions. In the previous section, we learnt that the conscious ego dissolves during the specialised conditions of meditation and tried to guess the "why" behind the ego's departure, but we did not bother engaging with the "how" of the matter; the *mechanism*—to say it the other way. In the section *Egoless-ness*, we explored the state that prevails in the absence of the ego, and here we shall see how this 'change' comes to be. Freud's view of the mind as 'dynamic' comes from the idea that different energies are in constant interaction in the mind, and the psychic life originates from their interplay. Continuing the same line of thought, there has to be a distinguished dynamic (energetic) arrangement when the world "appears" in the *hyle* phase, and the 'self' takes the backseat as a consequence.

The idea that the *'I'* requires a constant supply of energy for it to be nurtured by thoughts, memories, and familiar affective states has been validated by many thinkers. This view of the "self" being a creation of the consolidation that occurs amid the cusp of memories, affects, and thoughts can be witnessed during meditation and also has been bonafide by thinkers like William James and Husserl. "The stream of consciousness, with its continuous flux of experiences, is the absolute foundation on which all transcendent being is constituted".[1] The self-system is the pattern of attitudes, feelings, and values that give a sense of identity to the individual".[2]

Earlier, we learnt that the psyche has a provision of a *hyle* phase to occur, during which the empirical ego or the 'I' is absent, and the world appears in an essentially untouched and uncontaminated manner. In the previous sub-section *Egolessness*, we saw that the conscious ego may, in fact, have a feature of disappearing if 'appropriate' circumstances are provided. But there goes an *economy of energy* behind this "dissolution" to occur, and so in this section, I engage with the dynamic aspects of the psyche that make this 'dissolution' possible and make the world appear a little differently. In this discourse, I would like to point out beforehand that the term "libido" is borrowed from the Jungian lexicon instead of the Freudian. Where Freud understood the psychic energy—that the libido is—in a strictly sexual way; Jung, with his holistic and broader understanding of human nature and habituation in the world, considered libido the energy which is perceived as the motivating force behind all psychic activity.[3] In his elaboration, he refrained from further defining it and concludes by crediting it for being the fuel for every psychic function and human behaviour.

My imagination of this psychic energy powering different psychic entities is like that of a power grid covering the iceberg that the mind is. The source of origin for this energy is undoubtedly the Id. By "supply", I do not mean that it has the potential to bring those parts of the psyche to consciousness, let alone extend consciousness to them, but I mean that the energy brings those features to life and makes possible their functions to take place. In the absence of this energy, these systems are as good as non-existent, and the psyche would function without being under their influence. I propose the "I", just like any other psychic feature, thrives off this 'energy'.

In the previous section, we learned that the "I" dissolves under the appropriate conditions when the "will" (to meditate or to stay in the *hyle* phase) is employed. Jung called this "will" to be functional and credited its effectiveness to the psychic energy called the libido, which has the ability to make functional cum positional shifts in the psyche.

The ordinary psychic life is such that a portion of the libido is dedicated to the attitudes and orientations that effectively deal with the environment without any malfunctions, but as soon as any demand for a positional shift is felt, the libido supply is put at a halt, and the alternate orientation is powered.[4] In our case, the will to "see the world as purely as possible" is the cause of alterations in the ordinary psychic arrangements—which invariably has the provision for an "I" that observes. So now for a *hyle* phase, the libido pauses to fuel the conundrum that comes in the form of internal dialogue, memories, affective states and consequently the 'self' (as we read earlier, that "self" is nothing but a constellation of the familiar affective states and memories). On top of this energy shortage, the psychic contents are also actively suppressed by the 'will', ensuring the dissolution of the "I". The will, then directs the unattached libido to the sensory apparatus, causing a state of heightened awareness. Being now available for the senses, the libido expands the field of consciousness strictly in its orientation towards the environment. We also find evidence for this claim in modern psychological literature and research work. The idea of Willful Attention by John G. Nadra and George R. Mangun exactly resonates with my claims of free will.[5] In their study, they came to conclude that this voluntary attention is generated by the person internally, and is independent of the stimuli. On top of this, in brain imaging studies, it was found that attention caused by will is essentially different from the ordinary attentive states that rely on the nature of the stimulus. Brain imaging research has shown that voluntary, self-directed attention involves additional frontal cortical structures that interact with the brain's established attentional control networks, resulting in a modified network organisation for attention. Though there is no available literature, I would like to hypothesise that alongside the increased activity in the pre-frontal cortex, there must be a significant decrease in the lower parts of the brain—which would prove that there indeed is a reduction in other psychic functions—now that the libido is being directed to the consciousness. The limitations of this neuro-psychological research are reached when it cannot claim for certain if the activation in the pre-frontal cortex is due to heightened sensory awareness or an increase in other higher-order mental functions. But I can substantially claim that this increased activation has to be due to a more active engagement with the senses, as the pre-frontal cortex too is involved in a reciprocal relationship with sensory processing[6]; and so do the accounts of Phenomenology support, that there is no internal interference when a person engages with the world while maintaining *hyle*—including thoughts and other such higher-order functions. A landmark study by Mihaly Csikszentmihalyi (1975) on a different psychic arrangement (not Hyle) called the "Flow"[7], also substantially talks about a loss of the sense of self during certain states of profound engagement with a mental task, or a skill execution—called the state of Flow. Talking about this state is not of relevance to us here. Still, it nonetheless is a validation for the claim that I make here: "I" requires libidinal cathexis for its maintenance and ceases to 'be' as soon as the supply is paused on the occasion of a critical psychic event—requiring an essentially different dynamic arrangement.

References

1. Husserl, Edmund, Ideas: A General Introduction to Pure Phenomenon pg 102. Translated by W. R. Boyce Gibson. New York: Humanities Press INC., 1969

2. Sullivan, H. S. (1953). *The Interpersonal Theory of Psychiatry*. W.W. Norton & Company.

3. Jung, C. G. (1960). On psychic energy. In H. Read, M. Fordham, & G. Adler (Eds.), *The collected works of C.G. Jung* (Vol. 8, pp. 3-66). Princeton University Press. (Original work published 1928)

4. Ibid. pg 52

5. Nadra, J. G., & Mangun, G. R. (2023). The idea of willful attention. *eNeuro, 10*(6), ENEURO.0258-22.2023. https://doi.org/10.1523/ENEURO.0258-22.2023

6. Grujičić, R., Sedmak, G., & Nedeljković, U. (2023). The interplay of prefrontal cortex and sensory processing in perception and behavior. Frontiers in Psychology, 14.

7. Csikszentmihalyi, M. (1975). *Beyond boredom and anxiety: Experiencing flow in work and play.* Jossey-Bass

Chapter Four

Collective Synthesis

I think greater clarity and precision in understanding await us if we introduce the Freudian lexicon to this matter. Freud's formal thoughts on *Narcissism,* give out a similar model of energy dynamics where he suggests that there is a constant tussle between the external world (object cathexis) and the ego (ego cathexis) to gain a more significant share of the libido.[1] He explores multiple pathological conditions that originate from various dynamic libidinal arrangements: *Schizophrenia, Neuroticism* and *Narcissism,* to name a few.[2] He also states that the ego, in fact, is in need of the libido and is its primary site of demand. Freud acknowledges the limitations of working with the question of this dynamic energy and its utilisation, as it is neither easy to grasp nor sufficiently rich in content. For a substantial claim to be made, Freud could not possibly find any other site of observation, other than pathologies. I believe that my observations of meditation and Phenomenological concepts are the missing link that Freud would have benefited from and could have formally come to present a "scientific"—as he liked to call his endeavours—theory of the libido with greater substance. What is of our interest is the *'I'* and its possible connection with the libido and its dynamic relation with the external world. Freud states that there is a constant tussle between the ego libido and the object libido. And it takes the form of psychic conditions such as love or schizophrenia. If I were to trace the conscious "I" on the highly fertile grounds—of psychopathology—that Freud provides in the explanation of the libido, it would not be quite right, primarily because *'I'* is just a fraction of the ego. Secondly, the absence of it (strictly of the conscious aspect of it) is not a 'typical' psychotic experience (at least in its categorisation). Let me explain this further; though Freud, in his paper on *Narcissism,* does not explicitly state this, *Depersonalization* as a condition is developed by this very dynamic nature of the libido—that I have been discussing here—by depriving the ego (the entirety of it) of the libido and directing it to the external objects (this may seem same as *epoche,* but is not, let me explain). On the other extreme, we have *Schizophrenia,* where the libido is trapped inside, so much so that there is a loss of reality and absolute withdrawal from the world. Away from these, the ordinary psychic arrangement is preserved by maintaining an adequate balance between the internal and the external world. It would be only expected for one to doubt what makes the momentary disappearance of the *"I"* while not falling into a pathological state. The answer is that the disappearance of the conscious self is not a symptom of a cease of the ego (as it continues to persist in the deeper layer of the mind), and on top of this, *epoche* cannot be categorised as a psychotic experience because the ability to reestablish communication with the deeper fractions of the mind is still intact and is never given up as in the case of *Depersonalization.*

It would not be of benefit for this work to engage with the controversies between Jungian and Freudian thought on the *libido,* but if the reader wants to trace these claims of mine in the classic psychoanalytic literature, they should know that I personally stand more towards Jung, while agreeing with Freud that a pause in the libido supply can cause dysfunction in the psyche—a halt in the momentary genesis of the conscious ego—as it is the matter of our interest.

Collective Synthesis

We began with separately testing out two possible characteristics of the ego, namely:

- The conscious ego dissolves during certain moments, compromising the communication between different fractions of the mind, leading to an unordinary psychic arrangement. This line of thought was further enriched by observing the ego in meditative states and accounting for people's experiences of it. Though initially, we began with our entry point being "How does the world appear when there is no 'I'?", but through the way, we also ended up discovering "What happens when the ego dissolves?" as we searched for evidence for the ego's absence during meditation.

- Our second aim was to know if there is a dynamic reliance of the ego or of the 'I' on the libido. We found multi-disciplinary evidence for the possibility of a "selfless" state. We learn that there has to be a constant state of familiar affect and texture of experience and a two-way relation with the memory systems for the 'I' to be maintained. So, it is deduced that the "I" is the genesis of a psychic arrangement, the sustenance of which requires energy, and during compromised conditions, the essential energy is deployed elsewhere, making the 'I' disappear until the conditions persist.

I had begun by considering these two characteristics of the ego as independent of each other, but as we went deeper into them, we found consistencies in these supposedly independent features. While the first feature is limited to the dynamic arrangement that the 'self' is—not taking into account the economics of the situation, the second one explains the mechanism behind it.

A typical meditation experience is different from *epoche*, as it withdraws the attention from the environment, making the practitioner focus on the inside alone, while *epoche* halts the self from flooding the environmental experiences; both of these situations teach us about the exact same characteristic of the ego: its impermanence in the consciousness—as of now in the text—which makes us doubt our popular academic views of the psyche and the ego functions. It is held that the ego has been present in psychic functions right since its inception. I am leaving this aspect of the research at this point with the hope of finding practical implications of this newly found knowledge, which goes against our current psychological understandings and practice in the field. Here in these two highly specialised conditions, the *conscious ego,* perhaps on command of the *unconscious ego,* flees consciousness, letting the sensory apparatus be as transparent as possible—even of its own monitoring. If we recall, the genesis of the ego happens to handle the consciousness and serve the Id, while maintaining a balance between the two, but in neither of these states is the Id directly exposed to the environment, making them distinct from any forms of uncontrolled pathologies.

This makes us learn about the ego in an un-stereotypical way and enhances our knowledge of the boundaries of the ego. In my elaborate research, I learned that there is a positive future for this novel idea. I am optimistic about the possibilities that await us in our future studies on the ego and its possible contributions to understanding distinctions between ordinary psychic states and psychopathology. The ego has never been described or studied primarily through its absence. The states that occur after its departure are not pathological but are very much a provision of the psyche, both to observe the world in an uncontaminated way and to let out the otherwise repressed undercurrent, which is not allowed to be entered into the conscious due to the defences of the ego.

*

References

1. Freud, S. (1914). On narcissism: An introduction. In J. Strachey (Ed. & Trans.), *The standard edition of the complete psychological works of Sigmund Freud* (Vol. 14, pp. 67-102). Hogarth Press. (Original work published 1914)

2. ibid

Section B: The Body

Chapter Five
Body Ego

A human begins to navigate the world as a cluster of forces and conflicts. The biological arrangement that the human is—has to have faculties that help it navigate its environment effectively and purposefully. According to a widespread view in psychology, the movements the organism makes are prevented from being just chaos, credited to the mental faculty called the *ego*. Popularly, we know of the *ego* as a psychic entity that works to organise our experience and psychic content in cohesion so they do not form mutual conflict. The current order in academia at the intersection between stem disciplines and Psychology is dominated by the belief that the mental functions—handled by the brain—exist only in service of the human body's complex biological arrangement. Contemporary thoughts of *Determinism*, *Behaviorism*, *Neuroscience*, *Biopsychology*, and *Biopsychosocial-logy* keep the body and its survival at the core of the psyche's orientation and purpose of existence. We find traces of these inclinations in the early history of Psychoanalysis, in the writings of Freud, and in the history of General Psychology. Early psychologists must have felt the need to present themselves to academia as thinkers who abided by principles and had a scientific orientation, so they strived to position themselves in complement to biology and, therefore, hesitated to ever go against the grain. Freud situated his entire Psychoanalytic thought on the belief that humans are driven by the *Pleasure Principle* and defined this principle as a strive to fulfil our bodily needs of food, sex, survival, etc. This happened because of Freud's wish to establish Psychoanalysis as a scientific method to study the mind and place Psychology among natural sciences. I feel grateful to say that Freud, through his career, the developmental journey of psychoanalysis, and most notably through the persistent study of the mind, gained enough confidence to go against the dominant scientific understanding of the time and went *Beyond the Pleasure Principle.* Towards the end of his life, he introduced the *Death Drive,* which contradicted not just his own views and established concepts, but more importantly, no other human science had any space for accommodating anything like this that challenged their view of the human as a being that strives only towards survival and pleasures[1]. Most modern-day biologists try to tackle issues like suicide and self-harm by blaming them on faulty genes, 'atypical' neurobiology or environmental factors. In all these attempts, there is a wish to localise the cause of these tendencies by blaming them on specific factors so that their greater narrative of the human being as a pleasure-seeking organism is not threatened.

For this chapter, I would extensively cite Didier Anzieu, who begins his landmark work on *The Skin Ego* by explicitly stating that he wants to create a model that is solidly based on biology. My dissatisfaction with limiting oneself to the known plains of contemporary natural sciences is that we let go of our freedom to flirt with thoughts and abstract matters and lose our ability to produce novelty. I will revisit this argument in the next section; for now, let's talk about 'body'.

The body is essential as it is not only the host for the mind but also the hub of erogenous zones that play a critical role in the development of the personality, as the hunger of the erogenous zones has an influential role in human life. Philosophies like Hedonism, Aestheticism, and, most importantly, our personal life orientation encourage us humans to seek pleasure and avoid pain—it is not really a lesson that has to come from a recognised philosophy—mere observation of oneself may suggest this. 'Pleasure' seeking is just one tendency of the body—the senses in particular, and the greater purpose that they exist to serve is to act as receptors to the world around us.

For the first time, a sense of 'self' begins to form when a baby unfailingly receives people's reactions and treatment towards the infant body—that it 'is', and then intelligently deduces "I am something". Winnicott, in his *Maturational Process and Facilitating Environment*, states a hypothesis similar to what I just stated; the catch here is that the genesis of the self fundamentally arises from the perspectives of others.[2] It is in recognition of being subject to external forces beyond oneself that the affirmation of existence emerges:

"I am; because I am being held by something beyond my own being."

This formation of selfhood is rooted in the constraints of the corporeal vessel, consistently acknowledged and affirmed by those external to the individual, rather than by the individual themself. So, the body is essential for the ego and the self, not just because it is the origin of biological impulses but also because it is the mass that is both the subject and an object to the world. The psyche functions from different perspectives and makes use of the tools of the body, but it also observes the world constantly subjecting the body. All the internal pains and discomforts felt by the mind originate in the body, while the events happening outside the skin never appear quite as jarring—at least in non-pathological states.

This line of thought is the most dominant and has become the syntax for many theories; it also is the most adequate one for our exploration of the *body-ego.* Anything other than the body is deemed as "other", while the elements of the body are undoubtedly "my own". The sense organs become the meeting points of the inside and the outside, so they have a unique position in the mind—as the gateways from where the world enters. If it were not for the environment, the psyche would be left contentless and irrelevant. Interaction with the environment that goes on to constitute a significant portion of the psychic life begins within the small bubble of the infant-mother interaction, and its basic functioning can be learnt about from studying the baby's interaction with the mother, and the sense of corporeality in particular is to be credited to the mother's nurturance of the baby.

The entire body is of psychological significance, with each body part playing a role in maintaining the current shape of the psyche. The body, all the way from the hair, the nails, the genitals and the sweat, is recognised in the psyche, with each one having an influence on the individual—as a whole—as well as others during interpersonal contact. Dyeing of hair, painting nails, body art, skin tattoos and perfumes are all expressions of the psyche manifested on the body. Hair, in particular, secures a very ambivalent position in human life. Hair, in some situations, is considered gross and repulsive, but at the same time is an essential part of human intimacy and beauty. Psychological consequences of hair fall and baldness are proof of the significance of this dysfunctional component of our body called "hair".

By these examples, what I am trying to convey is that the body is not just a facilitator of the mind (as it contains the brain), but it also has a 'psychological worth'; its shape, condition and parts also have a metaphorical value for the mind and the way the psyche functions. Hinduism especially recognises how the environment interacts with the self and what body parts are of what significance in that interaction. The five fingers, for example, are associated with the 5 elements of the universe, each capable of channelising one element with a unique हस्त मुद्रा

(yogic hand postures). The thumb represents *Fire,* sensed with the *Eye;* the index finger represents *Air,* sensed through the *Skin;* the middle finger represents *Ether,* sensed through the *Ears;* the ring finger is associated with *Earth,* sensed through the *Nose;* the little finger is associated with *Water,* sensed through the *tongue.*

Psychoanalysis also recognises body parts and their vital role in expressions of fantasies, dreams and human traits. The mouth, for example, signifies nurturance, dependence, or devour of a love object—as expressed through a kiss. Anal, on the other hand, signifies control and orderliness. Teeth, in particular, have a unique role of delivering calculated hostility to the object being devoured (love object), as children often bite the breast that feeds them or as we chew the food in order to 'devour' it.

The body-ego is a vast subject in itself and can exceed the length of this text. For this reason, I shall deal with the "*Skin*" and "*Eye*". The reason for my choice will become evident in the course of this section, but their significance as sensory organs should be an adequate reason for this choice. The skin is the largest sense organ, while the eyes are arguably our most favoured sense organ.

*

References

1. Freud, S. (2015). *Beyond the pleasure principle.* Dover Publications.

2. Winnicott, D. W. (1965). *The maturational processes and the facilitating environment: Studies in the theory of emotional development.* The Hogarth Press and the Institute of Psycho-Analysis.

Chapter Six
The Skin

Religions for a very long time have been revising that it is the body and identification with the body, that is the origin of the 'ego'. Though this "ego" is intellectually distinct from what we are dealing with, it nonetheless was an intelligent claim to associate the ego with the body. Later, it was Freud, in the field of psychology, who firmly established the relationship between the ego and the body. He went as far as to state that "The Ego is primarily a Body-ego".[1] Freud's understanding of the dynamic psyche brought him to push out these statements, thinking behind which was that "the ego is born out of the Id to deal with the reality principle". We have engaged with this idea previously in the text, but since we are talking about gross matters in this chapter, let's understand this in more tactile terms. "The reality principle" does not only mean life circumstances that do not necessarily complement the Id's impulses, but the ego is also responsible for 'witnessing' the physical world, which appears to us through our sensory organs—the external 'reality'. This "witnessing" or "communication", as we may call it, happens through various scripts and pathways, and the script of the skin is the most primal and authentic.

This primal communication begins arguably even before birth when the baby resides inside the mother. It has been found that a sense of touch begins to develop in the fetus sometime during the 8th week, and from there on, the baby begins to react to different tactile sensations.[2] During this time, the baby lives in a cloud-like sensation that surrounds it; this sensation essentially is the first sensory communication between the mother and the child and continues to be relieved in moments of touch, hugs and the desire to be wrapped in clothes and wanting to sleep inside a heavy blanket. Though these are not universal wishes, nonetheless, they are significant wishes that are widely observed. Upon being born, the baby is made to receive skin-to-skin contact with the parents. Though there may be scientific claims like "regulation of body heat" as to why the baby is made to have skin contact with the parents, I say that there is something much deeper at play here. There cannot be a more accurate explanation as to why skin contact is necessary for the newborn other than the fact that it is humans' primary mode of communication. An orphanage observation in Romania held in the later part of the 20th century led to the learning that young children need something more than just nutrition and protection; a non-negotiable aspect of development and survival for mini-humans is physical touch.[3] "Children laid there as farm animals. No, they were worse than animals; at least animals dare to make noise." ~ the British observer Bob Graham noted.[4]

There is also vast scientific literature that is concerned with infancy and the need for touch. Most of the sites where children are kept in circumstances without their parents, become the site for observation of a common reaction of infants to lack of touch. An official at orphanages in the United States found that most children under the age of 2 years died despite having an ample amount of supplies and a protective environment; this biological condition was identified as precisely originating from a lack of human touch and was called "marasmus". Those children who managed to survive despite being touch-deprived developed emotional dysregulation later in their lives.[5]

'Childhood' is just one site of observation where human life can be understood in rather more straightforward expressions, but the importance of skin touch does not dissolve throughout our lives. Shaking hands, hugging, and fist-bumps are elements of social mannerism; no social interaction, in fact, is seen as 'normal' without there being some amount of skin contact. I hypothesise that **the degree of intimacy of a social relationship is determined by what form of skin contact is accepted and expected from a person.** If I were to stretch this logic to its limits, I **propose that people form social relations**

precisely to get touched—in manners that they deem appropriate—by the other person. (I do not mean that it is only 'touch' that we expect from people, but also 'play', relations of various natures, cooperation and much more. But since this chapter is dedicated to the 'skin', I shall talk only from this perspective). Just as in the case of childhood skin contact deprivation, we also have observations of adults who are deprived of human contact. Solitary confinement has been one of the most infamous punishments in human history. Prisoners who are punished with isolation obviously develop symptoms of sadness, but more than that is observable in the prisoners. Several studies and accounts highlight the development of psychopathology in prisoners subjected to solitary confinement.

A chapter in the book *Solitary Confinement: Effects, Practices, and Pathways toward Reform* discusses findings from a study of loneliness among long-term isolated prisoners, systematically assessing the prevalence of symptoms of psychological stress, trauma, and isolation-related psychopathology.[6] Another study titled *The Psychological Effects of Solitary Confinement: A Systematic Critique*, showed clinically significant symptoms of depression, anxiety, or guilt among half of the research sample, with disproportionately high rates of serious mental illness and self-harm behaviour compared with general prison populations.[7] An article titled *Psychopathological Effects of Solitary Confinement,* published in the American Journal of Psychiatry, suggests that social isolation may contribute to the development of mental illnesses, including schizophrenia.[8] The article presents a case where a patient was sentenced to isolation and was diagnosed with schizophrenia one year after his prison release. These accounts underscore the severe psychological impact of solitary confinement on prisoners, an issue that requires further research and consideration in the context of prison reform.

My bet here is that the skin as a body organ and the mental representations of it have contributions to the phase of ego development during the stage of infancy, and it has roles to play in maintaining ego cohesion throughout one's life. A deprivation of skin contact at any stage of life can be a valid factor for an incohesive ego, leading to emotional dysregulation, psychosis or even death. This was all for the skin ego's functions in relation to the environment—for maintaining the psychic functions, but there undoubtedly are a whole lot of functions that the skin ego has to execute—as we expect from the ego. In the following section, I describe the dual feature of the skin ego—the metaphor for the psychical representation of the skin—and how it becomes an instrument for self-preservation and self-expression. *Self-preservation* happens primarily by keeping the 'world' out and keeping the 'self' inside. The other function is concerned with letting the self 'get out' (self-expression) and letting the world 'get in'.

*

Reference

1. *Freud, S. (1923). The ego and the id. p.27 Hogarth Press.*

2. *Marx, V., & Nagy, E. (2015). Fetal behavioural responses to maternal voice and touch. PLOS ONE, 10(6), e0129118. https://doi.org/10.1371/journal.pone.0129118*

3. *Nelson, C. A., Zeanah, C. H., Fox, N. A., Marshall, P. J., Smyke, A. T., & Guthrie, D. (2007). Cognitive recovery in socially deprived young children: The Bucharest Early Intervention Project. Science, 318(5858), 1937-1940. https://doi.org/10.1126/science.1143921*

4. *The Borgen Project. (2019). The troubled history of Romanian orphanages. The Borgen Project. https://borgenproject.org/the-history-of-romanian-orphanages/*

5. *Chapin, F. S. (1915). Social evolution. The Century Co.*

6. *Lobel, J., & Scharff Smith, P. (Eds.). (2019). Solitary confinement: Effects, practices, and pathways toward reform. Oxford University Press.*

7. *Haney, C. (2018). The psychological effects of solitary confinement: A systematic critique. University of Chicago Press*

8. *Grassian, S. (1983). Psychopathological effects of solitary confinement. The American Journal of Psychiatry, 140(11), 1450-1454. https://doi.org/10.1176/ajp.140.11.1450*

Chapter Seven

The Pickled Self

> - *I experience; therefore, I am.*

The skin as a body organ serves functions like maintaining body temperature (psychologically speaking, "acclimatisation to the environment"), protection from unwanted illnesses, organisms, fungus, UV light and other environmental threats (synonymous with ego defences) and receiving sensations. In this section, I am going to explore the psychological significance of skin functions and how they contribute to maintaining the psyche, especially functions of the ego. By "maintaining the psyche", I mean the ordinary psychic functions responsible for "containing the self" that are otherwise taken for granted, as mental functions work by their own principles and have a whole mechanism at play behind the curtains.

Note: I may use "self" and "psyche" interchangeably in the upcoming sections, as I treat the 'self' as the whole of the psyche.

The Pickled 'Self'

The body is a jar that hosts the spicy self, which too, just like a pickle, would develop fungus if not preserved properly. The body, as the host of the psyche, acts as the breeding ground for numerous psychic functions, one of which is "containment of the self". We organisms navigate the world residing in our bodies, but this is not something to be taken for granted, as there has to occur a detailed sequence of milestones preceded by nurturance of the appropriate kind to be able to engage with the world.

The analogy of the 'container' and the 'contained' is an influential one among psychoanalytic thinkers. Thinkers like Melanie Klein and Wilfred Bion talk (in different contexts) about the "container" as a space that facilitates mental development and works as a host for emotional experiences. Enhancing Klein's analogy, Winnicott recognized the role of the mother's गोदी

(lap) as an essential space for the ego development of the baby.[1] Winnicott's theory paved the way for a tactile understanding of the analogy and helped us recognize the importance of visceral experiences necessary for ego development.

The skin, more than a barrier against the outside world, also houses all other sense organs and works to create harmony between different sensory organs as it helps the mind to knit a collective narrative out of them rather than attending to them independently. Sense organs sit on the skin on the peripheries of the body, serving the conscious self that resides as a collection of conscious appearances (in reference to the first section). With the development of motor controls, the child learns to command bodily movements and, in return, realizes that such command of will cannot be practiced on objects outside of the skin barrier. The skin becomes where the command extends up to, and it is here where the tactile world comes to meet the self on the borders of the skin.

Though all the sense organs are the meeting points of the world and the 'self', the skin holds a special place as it facilitates the most archaic forms of communication and sensorial experiences (with the mother, both before and after birth).

Note: From here-on, I proceed with the assumption that there is no need for me to formally establish the fact that people identify with their bodies—the 'self' is essentially the body itself. **My purpose here is to establish how the skin, in particular, helps to keep the sense of self and other psychic functions housed in the body, or how do skin sensations become part of the self in its current shape.**

The skin ego, if not formed properly, causes a whole lot of psychopathological complexities, such as Paranoid Terrors and the inability to be involved in sexual activities. Some sources claim even Borderline Personality issues have their origin in the maldevelopment of the skin ego.[2] Though there can be numerous explanations of the properties of the skin-ego, what follows is my explanation of it in concern to the momentary dynamics of the skin-ego—as a complement to my findings of the *conscious ego*.

I call this section *The Pickled Self* because the 'self' attains a certain flavor credited to being preserved in the container that the body is. Growing up a certain way, receiving creases for intimacies, pats for praises or hits as punishments, the human experiences life from the inside of the skin. Just as the skin is the site for pleasure (arguably), the most intense pleasures (as it includes sexual pleasures), it also is the site (arguably) for the most brutal punishments (as termination of the body is the ultimate death anxiety); and in both cases, the skin acts as the doorway for the environment to the 'self'. Experiences that enter through the skin not only shape the individual by providing one with a whole world of memories and orientations towards life (the 'pickled self') but also quite literally contribute to the creation of the current moment being experienced consciously.

A baby, when born, does not differentiate between the 'me' and 'not me'; it is only after repeated touches from the mother, sensation in different sites of this one unified lump of flesh—the body, and a spatio-temporal positioning of the body (especially the eyes), does one come to gain the understanding that the internal world and sensorial world meet at the playground called the body. The body is identified as an object different from all the other objects and people inhabiting the world, as it is the body—and—the body alone to which the motor commands can be practiced—as it alone becomes subjected to the wishes of the 'Will'. The significance of motor commands is that they become the instrument for environmental control and mastery. The inability to have command over events & people and not being aware of other people's experiences are the most influential factors in making a young human realize that their skin (as the outermost layer of the body) is till where their 'self' extends. I would like to emphasize my statement, "one's skin is till where the 'self' extends", and not the other way, "the 'self' is till the skin extends". For now, the reader need not get tangled up in the absurdity of this statement.[‡]

A child learns that people happen to hold different sensory experiences than their own self. Jean Piaget demonstrated this through his ideas of "perspectivism", where he claimed that after the age of 4, children begin to realize that different people may have perspectives distinct from theirs.[3] Though Piaget saw this purely with the aim of mapping out cognitive development, I claim that this development occurs on a tactile script of "learnt body habituation". The child learns that their experiences and perspectives are influenced by the body's spatial positioning; therefore, it is the body that hosts the entirety of their experiences.

---

‡ *I develop this idea in the next section of the book.*

If looked at from a classic Freudian perspective, the baby during the **Oral Stage**[4] realizes that the mother—more essentially, the breast is distinct from the 'self', and the 'self' gets to meet the breast at the oral site—skin of a different kind—**mucous membrane**. During this realization of 'not me', the baby also realizes the periphery of the self. Jean Piaget credited the understanding of 'me' and 'not me' to the first stage of Cognitive development. During the **Sensory Motor Stage** (age 0 to 2 years), a child gains "Self-Recognition", where the child develops aspects like bodily awareness, self-perception and physical recognition.[5]

Though Piaget does not state this, the child also learns that the periphery of the self is the 'skin'. Piaget said that this first stage is dominated by sensory-motor explorations, so I claim that rooted in senses, the child creates the 'self' on the carpet provided by the bodily sensations—the major chunk of which comes from the skin. In future, I would attempt to explore the concept of "Object permanence" (by Jean Piaget) from the perspective of skin contact, as babies grab objects—in the fist— in an attempt to preserve them from destruction, and how hand-holding in adulthood is reminiscent of the fear that "the object would cease to exist if I let it go away from my skin". The palm might have significant psychic worth, as it is extended out during social interactions, condolences and intimacy;[§] babies grab onto their parent's fingers, or in some cultures, the palm creases (हस्तरेखा) are believed to inform about a person's fate.

*

References

1. Winnicott, D. W. (1965). The maturational processes and the facilitating environment: Studies in the theory of emotional development. International Universities Press.

2. Anzieu, D. (1989). The skin ego (C. Turner, Trans.). Yale University Press.

3. Piaget, J., & Inhelder, B. (1956). The child's conception of space. Routledge & Kegan Paul.

4. Freud, S. (1905). Three essays on the theory of sexuality. In J. Strachey (Ed. & Trans.), The standard edition of the complete psychological works of Sigmund Freud (Vol. 7, pp. 123-246). Hogarth Press.

5. Piaget, J. (1952). The origins of intelligence in children. International Universities Press.

---

§§ *I speculate that just as a baby is wrapped in the womb, the palm becomes a recreation of the womb for the baby. Whether that be the palm of the mother or the self, clinching it brings reassurance. The palm is what is extended to people in social interactions. Fist in adulthood symbolizes determination. A closed fist is a hallmark of infancy. I speculate the fist is a mini womb.*

Chapter Eight
Canvas of the Self

The skin is not just a receptor for the outside world or a container for the internal self; it is an active medium of communication that "lets out" as well as "lets in." In the previous section, we discussed how the self is perceived as residing "inside" the skin. Now, let's explore how the skin acts as a canvas on which the self expresses itself.

Because the skin is the outermost body part, it is visible to others. In addition to its psychological value in ego cohesion and psychic well-being, the skin acts as a representation of the self to the outside world. The skin, by virtue of being the largest external organ, is observed by others and serves an important communicative role. This demarcation of the self is twofold: while the skin marks the boundary of the self, it also serves as the point at which others identify and recognize us.

The skin's surface indicates sexual fitness and is one of the primary markers of sexual attraction. Factors such as skin texture, facial redness, pheromones, and skin tone all play a role in sexual selection. Although there is ample research on the importance of appearance and its psychological impact, my aim here is to illustrate how the skin becomes a canvas for the self to be displayed. The skin serves as a tactile representation of the self to the world. For instance, occurrences like skin redness or sweating in social settings are believed to have psychological value and communicate a person's internal state. Similarly, scars, tattoos, blade marks, stitches, and piercings hold autobiographical significance, telling the story of a person's life and serving as records of experiences etched onto the body. I am reminded of a poem by contemporary poet Ashok Subramanian:

"Scars on our skin and minds are like the stars in the sky."

When you look at the stars in the sky, they appear as mere dots splurged across the dark fabric above us. Yet they twinkle and shine, each telling a story, speaking to us about our past, and inspiring us in the present. If our body is a universe, then the skin is the sky, and the scars are the stars.

~ Ashok Subramanian[1]

There also exists a Christian lore that tells of people arriving at the gates of heaven, where Saint Peter asks them to show their scars. Those who have none are asked, "Was there nothing worth fighting for?"

The belief that the skin is a canvas of the self has been evident in artistic expression for over 5,000 years. A corpse dating back to 3300 BCE, found near the modern Italy-Austrian border, had over 60 bodily inscriptions.[2] Tattoos and body art have long been used to display individuality and identity. Beyond permanent markings, temporary coloring, the use of cosmetics, and the modern obsession with skincare, all demonstrate the skin's immense psychological value and its crucial role in maintaining the ego.

These are conscious acts, all carried out with awareness. Tattoos, piercings, and scars are socially acknowledged ways of conveying one's story. These behaviors are learned and socially reinforced, becoming part of cultural expression. Another way to look at this is that these "marks" on the skin are externally caused but are imbued with psychological significance. Now, let's examine whether the psyche, specifically the ego, directly influences the appearance of the skin. As we proceed, I will explore the possibility that the skin serves as a site where psychic conflicts manifest.

While tattoos and scars overtly communicate the internal state of a person, there may be subtler, person-specific displays of psychic conflict that appear on the skin. Anzieu Didier, in his seminal work *The Skin Ego*, found a direct correlation between skin conditions like eczema, blushes, and rashes with specific ego states. He argues that such skin reactions have long been feared in gothic stories and modern fiction.[3] The field of psychodermatology, which builds on the principles of psychosomatics, has been engaged for years with skin diseases that arise in the absence of any biological cause, often requiring psychological intervention for resolution. While psychodermatology seeks to improve skin disease treatment, it also supports our claim that the skin is susceptible to psychic influence. But how does this convey anything about ego dynamics? For this, I will refer to a case study of a young woman who periodically develops rashes around her lips, a condition that has no known biological cause but is linked to a cluster of emotional experiences.

Ms. K, a young woman, has suffered from an undiagnosed skin condition for over seven years (as of 2024). She believes it is tied to a kiss she shared with a boy when she was in 10th grade. After kissing him, she developed irritation around her lips, which healed quickly after she took medication from a homoeopathic doctor. This first episode was forgotten, but when she kissed him once again a few days later, the condition returned—this time more persistently. Unlike the previous occurrence, which involved mild red marks, the skin now turned black, leading her to consult a dermatologist.

Her condition persisted for months, and she became so distressed that she continued using topical treatments for years. In 2022, after five years of continuous use, her mother forced her to stop the ointment and consult a new dermatologist.

This time, she was misdiagnosed with oral herpes. Dissatisfied with the diagnosis, she sought another opinion, and once again, the diagnosis was confirmed as herpes. Over the next several months, she took herpes medication, but her condition worsened, taking a toll on her mental health. Eventually, she returned to her previous dermatologist from 2017, who reassured her that she did not have herpes, and she was allowed to use the ointment that cured her initially. Even after seven years, both she and her doctors remain clueless about the biological cause of her condition.

While this is her medical history, there is a parallel psychological history. The boy she kissed was someone whom she despised, and she admits to kissing him "just for the sake of it". There was no emotional depth to the relationship, and she was quick to end it once she correlated her skin condition with the kiss. Over the years, whenever he has tried to reconnect with her, her skin begins to sting, leaving her in fear. The same thing happens if she ever encounters him in person or even in dreams. She always wakes up with redness and irritation around her lips, resembling the marks that appeared after kissing him.

What follows may seem dense, but it reveals a novel insight into the dynamic nature of the ego.

Robert Fliess, in his remarkable work *Ego and Body Ego*, introduces the concept of dividing the ego into two semi-institutions[4]:

- The **Partial Subject** (closer to the id)

- The **Introject** (closer to the superego)

Fliess formulates their roles through the lens of pathological states such as delusions, depersonalization, and hysteria. The Partial Subject represents impulses and desires, while the Introject is developed through the internalization of others' qualities into the ego. Both institutions operate in synergy, and when conflict arises, it can lead to ego splits or disorders like borderline personality disorder. The Partial Subject, being closer to the Id, is more primal, while the Introject represents socially acceptable morality.

What is particularly significant about the rashes and their location? The skin, as the host of erogenous zones, contains the Partial Subject, which resides at various locations, including the oral region. The recurring rashes seem to mimic the type that first appeared after her intimate encounter with the boy. She explains that her involvement with him was purely superficial, without any real affection. During this time, she was also subjected to criticism and shaming—what she describes as "slut shaming", by her classmates. She recalls that her 10th-grade year was especially difficult, as she became the "talk of the town," a situation that must have been emotionally taxing for her. The hostility and moral policing directed at her stemmed from her romantic choices, which she acknowledges her parents would never have accepted. This scenario, in my view, is a classic case of ego and superego conflict. The societal morality, internalized as the superego, likely caused guilt that her ego could not manage.

If we borrow from Fliess's concept of the two semi-institutions of the ego, we could argue that her Partial Subject (closer to the Id) and her Introject (closer to the superego) were in conflict. The kiss with the boy served as the tipping point. Her Introject (the internalized parental and societal morality) launched a hostile campaign against the Partial Subject (aligned with her bodily desires). The first time, the rashes were mild and light in color, but more painful than the subsequent outbreak. However, the second time she kissed him, the rashes, though less painful, were much more visible, so much so that she had to miss exams and wore a mask for several months. This escalation suggests that the punishment her superego inflicted on her the first time—aimed at preventing future engagement with the boy—was insufficient. Initially, the punishment was more personal and concealable, focused on her sensory experience (pain). However, when she ignored this and engaged with the boy again, the second "punishment" took a different form, one that was more humiliating and public. The black marks around her lips served as a form of "branding," a visible reminder of her transgression.

In this case, her superego's retaliation was not only to prevent her from acting immorally again but also to prevent others from engaging with her by marking her as "tainted." The first punishment targeted her directly, in the form of pain, while the second targeted her social appearance, branding her as a deterrent to others, the aim of which was 'humiliation'. Her Partial Subject and Introject were engaged in a dynamic battle, with the physical manifestation of the rash as the evidence of their conflict.

To summarize, the skin functions both as a protective barrier and as a canvas for self-expression, allowing the psyche to project its internal states onto the body. It houses the Partial Subject and serves as a stage where conflicts between the id, ego, and superego play out. Whether through conscious choices such as tattoos or unconscious reactions like rashes, the skin reflects the deep psychological forces at work within an individual.

References

1. *Subramanian, A. (n.d.). Scars on our skin and minds are like the stars in the sky. Retrieved from https://author-ashok.medium.com/poem-review-scars-ce259f9d31d7*

2. *Encyclopaedia Britannica. (2024). Ötzi. In Britannica. Retrieved from https://www.britannica.com/topic/Otzi*

3. *Anzieu, D. (1989). The Skin Ego (C. Turner, Trans.). Yale University Press. (pp. 153 & 310)*

4. *Fliess, R. (1961). Ego and Body Ego: Contributions to Their Psychoanalytic Psychology. International Universities Press.*

Chapter Nine

The Eye Ego

If I were to speculate based solely on my personal experience and observation of others, I would claim that the eyes hold the highest place in the hierarchy of sense organs. The world is filled with tactile objects experienced through the skin, but awareness of them can also be gained through visual observation—without requiring the observer to be in physical proximity to the object(s). Navigating the world—one of the ego's functions—requires continuous engagement with one's surroundings. The brain receives around 11 million bits of information per second from the outside world. The eyes sense the largest fraction of this: 10,000,000 bits, followed by the skin: 1,000,000 bits; the ears: 100,000 bits; the nose: 100,000 bits; and the tongue: 1,000 bits.[1] Out of the 12 cranial nerves, five are dedicated to the functioning of the eyes (CN II to CN VI).[2]

Our concern here, however, is the 'eye' not just as a sensory organ, but as a metaphor for physical orientation to the spatiotemporal world, an artistic element, and a tool of communication. Psychoanalysis allows us to acknowledge the possibilities of fantasies and their role in bridging the internal and external worlds that constitute the psyche, the world, and other psyches. The *Eye Ego*—the same as *The Skin Ego*—is a "phantasmatic reality". The eye, as a symbol, has appeared throughout human civilizational history. The Egyptian civilization had the eye of Horus, and Mesopotamians built temples dedicated to the human eye. Ancient Greece developed the apotropaic eye as a symbol to ward off evil stares.

The Roman civilization, for example, had the 'Evil Eye' symbol engraved on amulets and mosaics. This amulet's relevance persists today, as it continues to be worn on people's bodies or hung-over valuable objects. The reader may have encountered the symbol themselves—a blue disc with a black dot in the middle. Its sustained relevance stems from its perceived efficacy. The term "evil eye" has an equivalent in Hindi: नज़र,

which literally translates to "gaze." The superstition of the evil eye rests on the neurotic fear that others' malevolent intentions can influence one's life, with the gaze being the vehicle of its execution. This neurotic fear taps into the archaic belief in the omnipotence of thought. From this, we derive two key characteristics of the ego:

1. The ego extends to 'cover' infantile beliefs in omnipotence, necessitating defenses against the perceived omnipotence of others (i.e., the fear of the evil eye is actually a projection of one's own feelings of jealousy[3]). The ego architecture, perhaps,

extends up to the same psychic system that was designed to hold the belief of the omnipotence of thought. Demonstration of this possibility is that the ego employs defences against other people's omnipotence — the evil eye.

2. The ego employs defenses against others' omnipotence through mechanisms such as the evil eye. The eye, as an organ, is believed to possess uncanny powers. Being in the gaze of someone with an evil eye is thought to have the potential to cause actual psychic harm—bad luck. In contrast, physical violence through the skin requires two bodies to come into direct contact, but the eye can inflict harm without such physical proximity.

Both the above-stated characteristics of the ego—its defense against superstitious fears and its special connection to the eye—are also evident in clinical observations. Aside from Freud's remarks about the "evil eye" in *The Uncanny*, he notes in *Totem and Taboo* how paranoid projections stem from primordial fears of being watched by an evil eye.[4] Paranoid-schizoid patients often avoid eye contact, perceiving it as hostile.[5] It has been found that patients with paranoia describe their delusions of persecution as "constantly being watched" or "their eyes are always on me". While I do not intend to merely piggyback on established clinical literature to support my claims about *The Eye Ego*, these observations reinforce my argument that the eyes hold a special designation within the psychic, especially concerning the ego.

"The eye symbolises the force which levels an accusing look at the patient and reveals his inmost secrets."
~ Otto Fenichel, *The Psychoanalytic Theory of Neurosis* (1945)[6]

The Eye Ego—as noted in the previous section—finds its roots in the clinical and cultural significance of the eye. Well-established superstitions like the evil eye, and clinical phenomena such as paranoia, highlight the special role the eye plays in fantasies, cultural symbols, and fears. However, this only begins to suggest the Eye Ego as a legitimate metaphor for an aspect of the ego connected explicitly to the eyes. To fully understand the Eye Ego as a critical psychic element, we must explore how it unfolds.

When studying the genesis or basic characteristics of any psychic element, infancy offers a wealth of knowledge. During this period, psychic features are in relatively simple forms. Object relations theory, particularly in psychoanalysis, asserts that the interaction with the mother is fundamental in shaping the infant's ego. A nurturing environment provided by the mother is essential for healthy psychic development. In the earliest stages of life, when the baby is little more than a "lump of flesh" without a sense of self, it is the mother's eye contact that initiates the baby into subjectivity and intersubjectivity.[7] Eye contact is not just a simple sensory experience; it is crucial in the development of subjectivity and intersubjectivity. Just as the skin is vital for psychic development, so are the eyes. The mother's gaze helps regulate the baby's emotions and fosters attachment. The baby engages with the mother not only orally but also through the entire body—specifically, through the eyes. Varieties, for example, consider the first creature they see upon opening their eyes to be their mother.

References

1. Encyclopaedia Britannica. (2024). Information theory: Physiology. In *Britannica*. Retrieved from https://www.britannica.com/science/information-theory/Physiology

2. Healthline. (n.d.). 12 cranial nerves: Functions and diagram. Retrieved from https://www.healthline.com/health/12-cranial-nerves

3. Freud, S. (1919). *The uncanny.* In J. Strachey (Ed. & Trans.), *The Standard Edition of the Complete Psychological Works of Sigmund Freud* (Vol. 17, pp. 217-256). Hogarth Press.

4. Freud, S. (1913). *Totem and Taboo: Resemblances between the Psychic Lives of Savages and Neurotics* (A. A. Brill, Trans.). Moffat, Yard and Company.

5. Smari, J., Overill, J., Stefansson, S., & Ehrenberg, S. (1994). *Paranoid Ideation and Social Anxiety in Normal Subjects: Their Relationship with Interpersonal Perceptions and Behavior.* European Journal of Personality, 8(2), 75-82.

6. Fenichel, O. (1945). *The Psychoanalytic Theory of Neurosis.* W. W. Norton & Company.

7. Beebe, B., & Lachmann, F. M. (2002). *Infant research and adult treatment: Co-constructing interactions.* The Analytic Press/Taylor & Francis Group.

Chapter Ten
Ego Nucleus

-   I see myself, therefore I am.

By now, the reader must have learned that the ego, as a psychic feature, comes to be formed through a process and does not just happen to exist by fluke. In the previous section *The Skin*, I initiated my proposal by laying out the popular understanding of ego and the biological reason for its genesis. Me telling the reader about the bodily origins of the ego had three reasons: to acquaint the reader with a relatively simpler and popularly accepted understanding of the matter; to provide you with a lamp to walk the path I was about to take you on; and thirdly to demonstrate to the rather rudimentary reader (who possesses their knowledge on the ego from non-psychoanalytic sources) that the author of this book is aware of the popular understanding of the ego in contemporary psychology. The bodily origin of the ego is true but unlikely to capture the entire reality or magnitude of this feature. For that, let's try to breach the orthodox understanding of ego formation.

Beginning now, I expect the reader to have an awareness of the psychoanalytic opinion on ego development, especially the perspective of Winnicott, Anzieu, and Lacan. I am refraining from restating them and am instead sticking with their line of thought to build my own ego system. Just as the tactile holding of the mother is given recognition or the essential act of first lovemaking with the breast is recognised as an unavoidable step towards a baby's development, eye contact too is one of the cornerstones of mother-child relations.

I personally have observed a trend among psychoanalytic thinkers that they either try to confine the entire process of ego development to the bodily nurturance that the baby receives or they take an entirely opposite view on this and limit the ego to the status of an entity built by intellectual milestones achieved in the course of life.** British psychoanalysts like Klein and Winnicott valued the nurturing quality of relations experienced in early life and considered them vital for the development of a cohesive ego. While I personally think that their abidance to the bodily realities as the foundation of their thoughts came from a lack of confidence in their discipline, so the boundaries they limit themselves to are strictly biological. The outline of their frame of thought is limited to the "scientific" knowledge of their time, and while reading their work, it becomes evident that they were cautious about not going against the grain—biological literature of their time. The

---

** I further develop this argument in "Ego Architecture", added in the Appendix section.

French psychoanalysts were radical in their own regard and were able to liberate themselves from the shadow of biology, but all they knew was the ego—at its core—as a faculty of the intellect. According to Lacan, upon seeing himself in the mirror for the first time, the baby is filled with intense emotions and it is this episode that serves as the founding of the ego.[1]

"We have to understand the mirror stage as an identification... the transformation that takes place in the subject when he assumes an image."
~ Lacan, 1949.[2]

While both these distinct thoughts have added to the psychological discourse, this cleavage in the literature becomes evident when one tries to build an all-comprehensive compilation of the subject matter. Just as the tactile holding of the mother is given recognition or the essential act of first lovemaking with the breast is recognised as an unavoidable step towards a baby's development, to my dissatisfaction, there is little to no mention of the eye contact that the mother and child engage in. The infant indulges in a relatively simple back-and-forth relationship with the mother, the mediums of which are few. Along with the mother's warmth and bodily nutrition, the baby is also reliant on the visual verification of her perpetual presence. Eye contact, despite being one of the cornerstones of mother-child relations, is not emphasised enough in popular psychoanalytic literature. Even the literature on Attachment theory that does talk about the psychological significance of this does not see it as an attention-worthy exchange in its own regard.[3]

Winnicott credits the "good enough mother" for the baby's ego being a strong one. It is the interaction with the good enough mother, who provides the baby with an experience of omnipotence, that facilitates the nurturance of an ego that is cohesive enough to face life circumstances in the future.[4] The mother temporarily dedicates herself to the baby and ensures the baby is minimally left alone to face the dread of existence, if at all. The baby's needs are met by the good enough mother as soon as they emerge, making the baby feel that he can summon anything he wishes. What psychoanalytic thinkers miss is that the baby has to identify the source of these gratifications, the tool for which is only one—visual verification. The baby, as a blob of mass, cannot quite make sense of any physical sensations—touch predominantly. The baby develops an active relationship with the mother instead of being at the receptive end of the biological duty of the mother. The relationship is ideally built on love, with several streams of communication and affection active at the same time. Physical touch and proximity, a consistent odour, voice, and eye contact, among many others, are the elements of any relationship that a person ever forms in one's life. The architectural design for any relation that a person develops in their life is formed in their infant state with the mother. During this period, the baby's vision has a special place in his experience of the world and the caregiver. The mother and the child engage in eye contact as a mode of communication with a relatively simple script of this exchange. Generally (though not always), active eye contact is rewarding for both the mother and the child, while the absence of eye contact is anxiety-provoking for both. A study from 2002 demonstrates that infants as young as 2 days can identify human gaze and prefer to maintain eye contact with the faces that are actively looking at the baby.[5] A separate study from Cambridge University, published in 2017, claims that eye contact helps create synchronisation in the baby's brain and body with that of the adult.[6] This puts across my claim of the psychological significance of the functions of the eye as a biological organ but does little to establish the Eye Ego as a valid fraction or even as a metaphor for the ego as we know it. For that, let's trace the development of the ego afresh. The model that I am going to propose is constructed through a retrospective analysis of the ego—as it is observed in adult life. I must inform the reader that what I am going to present to you is neither the architecture of the ego nor exactly its history of development. I claim that the experience of being inside one's head is actually the experience of being behind the eyes.[††] The eyes, as the primary source of information from the outside world, have a special status in our psyche reserved only for them. A newborn meets his mother not just at the oral site but also at the eyes, making the eyes a site of exchange—just as the skin. While the mother's gaze towards the baby is reassuring, the baby's gaze is joyous and rewarding for the mother. The duo engaging in a mutual gaze is the first communicative exchange that, for the baby, sets a premise for the life to come. The experience of being looked at is of the same कोटि of reassurance as the mother's गोदी. Winnicott tells us that at this young stage of life, the baby is at all times at the brink of "unthinkable anxiety," kept at bay only by the mother's reassuring presence and care. Among the four varieties of this "anxiety" is one: "having no orientation." This primal anxiety can be dealt

---

[††] *For many years, this observation has been re-occurring to me that people live with a subconscious belief that they "inhabit" the body. This idea may seem distant to the reader who has been a student of psychology for a considerable period of time, but if you try, you might be able to extract from a layperson that they reside in their body. People often speak in ways that convey their idea that their 'self' (a spirit) is inside their body, usually in their head. Often, this feeling is translated as "It is the brain that I am inside of", but actually, that is just a poor comprehension of a much greater psychological experience that directly relates to the nucleus of the ego. With the hope that I have communicated (if not entirely convinced the reader of this phenomenon), I proceed. Every psychological experience has to have an origin and a probable explanation, especially when the one being discussed is related to the phenomenology of the self.*

with only in the care of a good-enough mother, who looks after the baby's body—primarily through tactile modes of affection. Winnicott pays primary attention to the act of holding the baby, which in his understanding is a form of love that can be shared between the two. He states, "Holding includes especially the physical holding of the infant, which is a form of loving".[7] Both psychoanalytic thoughts of the primary and sole relation between the infant and the mother being bodily; "the baby meeting the mother (the breast) at his oral site" and "the baby being dependent on the mother's act of holding" present the baby as a passive participant in the relationship. But actually, the baby is the cause of change in the mother's life and also acts as an active participant in the relationship instead of just being an accumulation of cells and a source of nuisance. The child and the mother engage in a series of communicative exchanges.[8] During infancy, when psychology has not yet emerged from physiology, there is no symbolism, and the only reality is bodily. So, all the distress that we can assume occurs to the infant is physiological. Having no orientation, which may be experienced in adulthood as a cluster of psychological cluelessness accompanied by psychopathologies of the serious kind, stems from the disorientation an infant may experience if there is a lack of care from the mother. Winnicott sums up all possible protection against this unthinkable anxiety with a general term he calls "holding." By virtue of having come up with the metaphor of the *Eye Ego*, I am confident in proposing that the fear of having no orientation is, and can only be, dispersed by the mother's gaze and the baby's acknowledgment of it. In other words, not having to deal with a lack of orientation in one's life is a result of receiving adequate eye contact from the mother. I credit Winnicott for acknowledging that the sense of self is developed in the baby when he observes people 'looking' at him and intellectually deduces that there is something these people are looking at. Hence, the sense of self comes to be.

It is only expected that the reader, at this point, may wonder how a sensory quality of experience—vision—of being looked at helps induce the ego. There are multiple reasons why the eyes come to hold this special position; let me explain them by putting them in a sequence (just for the sake of comprehension).

First, in the experience of being looked at, it is the sight of the person's gaze that becomes crucial for the development of the self. While the mother looks at the baby, she primarily looks at his eyes. The experience of engaging in intimate eye contact with the mother acts as an element of her "holding," protecting the baby from what prevails otherwise by acknowledging the baby's existence as significant. As a result, the baby develops an 'idea' of the 'self' residing somewhere behind his eyes. I should repeat that it is just an intellectual deduction of having the 'self' being somewhere behind one's eyes and not an absolute entity. This is the same impression that one ordinarily carries throughout life of being 'inside' their head. This is quite similar to what Winnicott calls "Psyche indwelling in the Soma"—the realisation that the psyche is 'inside' the body.[9] This realisation comes from a linkage between sensor-motor and functional experiences of the body. With this, the baby also begins to distinguish between 'inside' and 'outside'.

The act of the mother communicating with her facial expressions and yet-incomprehensible words while looking at the baby 'inscribes' a 'self' in the baby. Like any other internalisations and identifications that the baby develops from the mother or the primary caregiver, the baby also internalises a sense of self that lies behind her eyes.

Second, the learning of being a unit in oneself becomes possible only through the faculty of vision (of course, I am talking while considering a person with the faculty of sight as a prototype). The body, as a cloud of sensations, never comes to be experienced as a cohesive entity except for when it is 'seen'. Lacan addresses this in the Mirror Stage when the baby, for the first time, 'sees' himself in the mirror and, as a result, experiences himself as a cohesive unit.[10] Vision provides the individual with information about the continuity and cohesion of their soma, like a psychic acknowledgment of one's existence.

The habituation of the body as one's own happens only after the visual knowledge of it is gained. Sensory-motor coordination is achieved only when there is visual feedback of one's actions. People who are blind also go through the same process; the only difference being that they have an adult accompanying them. For example, a child has to 'see' his hands to know that he has hands. If I could have the liberty to speculate, I assume that children who do not have the faculty of vision have to be 'taught' about their corporeal contours and functions by a caregiver; the coordination they have in their body happens through tactile means rather than visual. In normative cases, it is the visual recognition that lets a person build an 'idea' of corporeality. This intellectual acknowledgment of 'having' a body might be a key link in the psycho-soma connection that later becomes a person's entire reality.

Vision helps one gain awareness of 'being'. By "awareness of being," I mean the knowledge—gained through vision—of one's being, which is then cherished as the 'self'. If I carry this line of thought further, it suggests that the 'self,' as we know it in psychology (even the unconscious aspects of it), might actually be a constellation of elements built over time. If I were to speculate what this 'constellation' comprises, I would say that these are the observations of one's experiences and texture of being—just as the body was once 'observed,' so are other of its elements.

The real drift in my proposal is that the 'self' being a constellation is not just a cluster of picked-up things but rather a collection of reflections accumulated over time. Just as the visual awareness of 'having' a body is once gained early in life, so are its other aspects. What is being observed is not the 'self' as we know it, but the texture of being. And it is on this 'being' that the 'self' is built.

The above-mentioned constructed self, which both witnesses and is witnessed, acts as the epicentre for interaction with the world. These psychic developments of being "seen" (by) and "seeing" the outside world serve as the foundation of the ego. (I speculate) At the root of the ego is the ability to subject and be subjected by the world. The chaos that the mind is, develops the entity we call the "ego" to effectively navigate the world; this navigation happens by establishing two-way communication with the outside world. This correspondence between the self and world objects becomes possible only through the eyes, as they host the self that does both: to subject and be subjected. In my personal opinion—to an unknown extent—the self might actually be a localized phenomenon residing behind the eyes. The reason for this speculation is that during the early stages of life, psychology is subservient to physiology, and it is the body that serves as the real estate for the development of the self.

The reality principle faced in the absence of the ego causes senseless chaos that overtakes the individual and sways him like a dinghy stuck in strong ocean currents. A child without vision, too, must feel the same when bombarded with bodily sensations—the sources for which remain unknown. Worldly experiences are synonymous with bodily sensations, which, if met in the absence of the ego and vision specifically, leave the individual unoriented.

*

References

1. Lacan, J. (1949). The mirror stage as formative of the function of the I as revealed in psychoanalytic experience. In *Écrits: A Selection* (A. Sheridan, Trans., 1977). W. W. Norton & Company.

2. Ibid

3. Bowlby, J. (1969). *Attachment and Loss: Vol. 1. Attachment.* Hogarth Press.

4. Winnicott, D. W. (1965). *The maturational processes and the facilitating environment: Studies in the theory of emotional development.* International Universities Press.

5. Farroni, T., Csibra, G., Simion, F., & Johnson, M. H. (2002). Eye contact detection in humans from birth. *Proceedings of the National Academy of Sciences of the United States of*

America, 99(14), 9602-9605. https://doi.org/10.1073/pnas.152159999

6. Leong, V., Byrne, E., Clackson, K., Georgieva, S., Lam, S., & Wass, S. (2017). Speaker gaze increases information coupling between infant and adult brains. *Proceedings of the National Academy of Sciences, 114*(50), 13290-13295. https://doi.org/10.1073/pnas.1702493114

7. Winnicott, D. W. (1960). The theory of the parent-infant relationship. *International Journal of Psycho-Analysis, 41*, p 591.

8. Trevarthen, C., & Aitken, K. J. (2001). Infant intersubjectivity: Research, theory, and clinical applications. *Journal of Child Psychology and Psychiatry,* 42(1), 3-48. https://doi.org/10.1111/1469-7610.00701.

9. Winnicott, D. W. (2016). Dwelling of psyche in body. In *The collected works of D. W. Winnicott: Volume 11, Human nature and The Piggle* (pp. 139-142). Oxford University Press.

10. Lacan, J. (1949). The mirror stage as formative of the I function as revealed in psychoanalytic experience. In *Écrits: A Selection* (A. Sheridan, Trans., 1977). W.W. Norton & Company

Chapter Eleven

Love

-    *The eyes are the windows to the soul.*

The psychic trend of feeling acknowledged when being looked at, which once started during infancy, perpetuates well into adulthood. The frequency of eye contact that a person usually maintains has been found quite predictable in individuals with Autism, Depression, Social Anxiety, and poor interpersonal skills. Serving as a cornerstone for social interactions and the primary form of non-verbal communication (in situations that expect non-physical proximity), the eyes act as the representative of the self (for this context, let me remind you that the self is a product of the ego). The pattern of eye contact alone can be indicative of various mental conditions; it is not just in cases of psychopathologies, but a rather irregular 'eye behaviour' is also an expression of the 'ordinary' internal state—the ordinary self too, is to be found through the way of the eye. It does not require an expert's suggestion to tell the reader that the eye has a monumental role in personal expressions and the navigation of their social and interpersonal life.

The mother-child relationship serves as the blueprint for the baby's life that is yet to come. The eye contact in which the baby, once engaged with the mother, helps develop not just the self but also the foundation of love that one experiences in their life. The act of engaging in mutual eye contact—by the accounts of many—is the first step towards the beginning of intimacy. The act of gazing at somebody is an acknowledgment of their existence which, in ordinary circumstances (considering the people we are referring to have the faculty of vision), is unavoidable for an engagement to happen, let alone a relationship to be built. The experience of being 'seen' is that of being subjected to the other's self. A mutual engagement in eye contact between people puts both egos in a unique position which perhaps serves as the kernel for any human interaction and interpersonal relation of any kind—even hostility. When looking at another person, the ego is essentially performing one of its primary functions—to be extroverted—by subjecting the other's ego, while the other aspect of 'eye contact' is to be subjected by the other's ego. It is this correspondence that enables any communication between people. I would like to speculate that it is this dialectic that serves as the kernel for the spread of ideas, psychic experiences, empathy, psychological contaminations like psychopathology, and even sanity.

Independently of this work, I have been contemplating the possibility that 'sanity' is a social construct that is communicated among people. If we do not take the structure of the psyche or the ego for granted by crediting their relative uniformity among people all over the world—as an expression of biology, we may open doors to a new way of thinking about the mind. I hope to write about this sometime in the future, suggesting that the psychic organisation and the dynamic structures we possess and process-by might actually be introjections from the environment.[‡‡]

The dynamics of the mother-child relationship (specifically from the perspective of the Eye Ego) continue to dictate one's life in their romantic pursuits and intimacies. Just as the baby once used to reach for the breast with the intention of oral satisfaction, which later translates to stretching oneself out to kiss a lover (love object), the aspect of eye contact too stays alive, dictating one's life and longings. Just as a baby puts every object of interest in its mouth as an attempt to experience it as a part of itself (the ego devours its love object through the oral pathway), an adult cannot help but 'look' at the object of their interest.

[‡‡] I further develop this idea in *Ego Architecture* in the Appendix section of the book.

- Eye contact has the quality to be a non-tactile kiss.

Writing this reminds me of a Bollywood song, the lyrics of which are:

तेरे चेहरे से नज़र नहीं हटती, नज़ारे हम क्या देखें

तुझे मिलके भी प्यास नहीं घटती, नज़ारे हम क्या देखें

~ Sahir Ludhianvi[1]

While there is nothing extraordinary in these lyrics, they capture the helplessness of a lover to look away from their beloved, as they cannot resist looking at them. I cite this song primarily because it is hovering in my mind as I write about the desire to 'taste' someone by looking at them; secondly, due to the approval that songs like this have found among listeners, indicating that there is a general acceptance among people about carrying desires like this. The number of metaphors dedicated to the eyes is overwhelming. Another quite popular song written by Ravindra Jain[2] goes like:

अखियों के झरोखों से मैने देखा जो सांवरे

तुम दूर नज़र आए, बड़ी दूर नज़र आए

बंद करके झरोखों को ज़रा बैठी जो सोचने

मन में तुम्हीं मुस्काए, बस तुम्हीं मुस्काए

The phrase "अखियों के झरोखों से" signifies the window-like character of the eyes. This is the window through which one sees their lover. These lines from the song *Akhiyon Ke Jharokhon Se* capture both my observations: the self residing behind the eyes and experiencing the other through the eyes as a primal mode of experience — just like the oral site.

Hindi idioms like "आंखों का तारा" and English idioms like "Eye Candy" beautifully articulate the essence of the Eye Ego. These insights suggest that any degree of affection for someone fundamentally involves visual admiration, with the visual component (shaped by subjectivity) being a crucial element. This does not imply that only objective beauty can lead to someone being liked. Rather, it means that liking someone cannot be separated from visual admiration. The appreciation of the visual aspect may precede or follow the feeling of liking, but it likely always accompanies it.

*

References

1. Ludhianvi, S. (1976). Tere chehre se nazar nahi hatti [Song]. On *Kabhi Kabhie*. Saregama India Limited.

2. Jain, R. (1978). अखियों के झरोखों से [Song]. On *अखियों के झरोखों से.* Saregama India Limited.

Chapter Twelve

Empathy

The world, in general, has been arranged in a manner that requires the faculty of vision for navigation. Although the material world is suited for tactile sensations, the navigation of the spatial world requires the ability to 'see.' Language scripts, maps, entertainment, education (the spread of ideas), documentation, etc., have all been molded for sighted individuals.

The references mentioned until now are literary and represent artistic and intellectual interpretations of a psychic phenomenon. Eye metaphors, idioms, and poems resonate with the masses, but still, they only capture the agony or joy of a single soul—the individual. However, there is also a rich collection of material related to the Eye Ego in the performative arts. The philosophy of *Rasa* comes to tell us about the birth of *Rasa*, which is a co-creation of multiple egos. Performative arts, as designed to appeal to the faculty of vision, have a rich philosophy behind their genesis. Indian aesthetics are based on the aim of invoking certain aesthetic experiences in the audience–रस. As we

will learn now, the aim of invoking *Rasa* in the spectator is fulfilled by a correspondence built between the writer and the audience, also called *रसिका*. *Rasa*, by its nature, transcends the individual ego, as it is birthed only after the interaction of elements of both the art (written by a writer and represented by an artist) and the *रसिका*.

Indian performative arts like *अभिनय* and *नृत्य*, which use the body as a mode of expression, are very particular about the visual aesthetics of even the smallest body contours and movements. Performances like dance or theatrical acting may seem like a mere method of stimulation with participants—the performer and the audience— serving as the source and the recipient, but such is not the case. Art forms like these, with the visual mode as their choice of communication, rely on interrelational experience between the performer and the audience. Diving into the *Rasa* philosophy, carrying the frame of thought we have built so far—in regard to the Eye Ego—we will explore two themes. First, in regard to the expressive and demonstrative aspect of the eyes: *Netra Bheda*. The second theme is concerned with the dialectical relation established between the audience and the performer, the result of which is the birth of *Rasa*, which will be taken up alongside a psychoanalytic frame of thought in the succeeding section.

The *नाट्यशास्त्र*/*Natyashastra* emphasizes a calibrated use of eye gestures to invoke *Rasa* among the audience. Having a specific eye expression dedicated to different internal states, it makes use of the demonstrative aspect of the eyes. It works on the fact that the eye ordinarily behaves a certain way, which is mimicked during performances to establish a relationship with the audience.

Netra Bheda: Bharata's *Natyashastra* (Natyashastra written by भरत ऋषि) in particular mentions eight types of eye glances, while a compilation from other sources makes the total number reach forty-four, with each one having a distinguished meaning.[1] These eye gestures are used to express psychic states, with some of them capable of producing uncanny feelings in the viewers. Let me describe a few of them:

- *Sama:* Not blinking. Used to depict a godly woman.

- *Ullokita:* Looking upwards. Remembering past births.

- *Avalokita*: Looking downwards. Looking at one's own body or shadow.

- *Akasa:* Pupils rolled backwards. Witnessing things happening in the sky.

My purpose in selectively citing some of the glances is to create visceral experiences in the reader to communicate the palpable reality of the script on which 'eye communication' happens. None of these eye expressions are limited only to art forms but are components of daily living. *Sama* may paint an image of a performer embodying a demigod in the mind of the reader, but in my observation, people often engage in an unsaid competition of not blinking their eyes while maintaining eye contact, with an unsaid rule that the person who is able to outlast the other is superior. I speculate that endurance in maintaining eye contact is about having the power to handle the tension that accompanies the subjected-subjecting experience that arises while looking at someone and being looked at simultaneously. The performer who looks at the audience with a virtually unbroken gaze is considered divine as she is able to hold the tension that arises as a result of subjecting and being subjected by others.

Avalokita involves looking at one's own body or shadow, which perhaps is one of the most ordinary aspects of human life. I have already mentioned that the acknowledgment of oneself as a cohesive unit comes from a visual experience of the body. The aspect of having the 'shadow' as an element of the self—which too is being observed by the glance, called *Avalokita*—will be discussed in the next section of the book concerned with *'beyond the body'*.

Akasa & Ullokita: The reader may fail to make sense of these eye movements, as these are not commonly observed aspects of the human psyche. While people who have an experience of deep and rigorous meditation may immediately make sense of it, I would not abandon the unknowing reader without explaining the phenomenon. To explain the psychological significance of these eye movements, I shall refer to a case of schizophrenia mentioned in a dissertation written by one of my colleagues for her Master's.[2] One of the subjects of her study, Mukul, was taken as a participant due to his history of schizophrenia and was in remission at the time of the interview. About Mukul, she writes:

"He mentioned his eyes used to roll away or go backwards, but have stopped now. No further detail was provided regarding the same, except that it was a side effect of one of the antipsychotic medications, which were later corrected".

The experience of his eyes rolling backwards used to occur in the thick of his schizophrenia. Though he was at peace by blaming a drug named Soltus, my research shows no such side effects associated with the drug. The study is interested in the memories of the psychotic experiences of the participant. Hence, it does not particularly address what internal images or thoughts might have accompanied the 'rolling' upwards of the eyes. General information about the participant informs us that his schizophrenia involved reoccurring auditory hallucinations of "those whomever he had met," "of younger ones," and "of people." This is similar to what a performer on the stage might pretend to experience by rolling their eyes backwards. There is an uneasy and incomprehensible—yet palpable—similarity between a schizophrenic immersed in hallucinations and an artist (immersed in their character) recalling their past lives while being in a trance-like state of having given up their individuality at the cost of embodying the character's reality onto themselves.

Rasa

First understood in the नाट्यशास्त्र /*Natyashastra* written by Bharata Muni, the theory of *Rasa* has been influencing Indian arts. The theory of *Rasa Nispatti* addresses the birth of *Rasa*. *Rasa* is the aesthetic flavor experienced by the audience as a result of engaging with art. The process of *Rasa* genesis is not of a simple stimulus-response but of a dialectical kind. *Rasa*, an aesthetic flavor, comes to be experienced as a co-creation of four elements:

1. *विभावा/Vibhava*: Stimuli that evoke emotional responses in the character. This may include their circumstances and other characters in the story.

2. *अनुभव/Anubhava*: Bodily expressions of the performer to express the emotions being experienced by their character.

3. *व्याभिचारी भाव/Vyabhichari Bhava*: These are the fleeting states of mind of the character that the artist is performing. These can be understood as thoughts, dilemmas, nervousness, etc. They are not as stationary as *Sthayi Bhava* but play a complementary role to them to attain *Rasa*.

4. *स्थायी भाव/Sthayi Bhava*: The primary emotion that is evoked in the audience. Each *Rasa* is associated with a particular *Sthayi Bhava*; for example, *Shringara Rasa* (eroticism) is associated with *Rati* (love).

The theory of *Rasa Nispatti* works on a dialectic established between the performer—representing the story being performed—and the audience—carrying their own *Sthayi Bhava*. So, *Rasa* is not something that is 'caused' but co-created by the interaction between the *Kavya* (poem) and the audience. The medium of this communication remains visual, and in *Nritya*, due to the lack of dialogues, the responsibility of communication is entirely borne by the visual performance of the artist. Each body contour and sway has a meaning behind it. It may seem unfathomable, but objects like planets, gods, relatives, rivers, oceans, and animals are symbolized through just hand gestures. The audience is taken on an emotional journey with the artist through the course of the performance, the ultimate goal of which is to make them experience the *Rasa* that the writer of the poem intended them to. I must remind the reader that all this happens on the bandwidth of the visual faculty. Psychologically, it is the relatedness that the audience is able to feel with the character, along with active fantasies, that enable the aesthetic experience.

It would be great if by now, the reader is already expecting me to introduce a Psychoanalytic perspective to this, but I feel it would be of greater benefit if we just wait a little.

I believe it was an adequate introduction to Indian Aesthetics. The aim of presenting this was to provide the reader with a philosophical perspective on how a communicative relation built on the faculty of vision can take the spectator on a journey of experiences. I am not yet done giving a psychological perspective on this. But for now, I should conclude this chapter.

Reference

1. Coomaraswamy, A. K., & Duggirala, G. K. (1917). *The mirror of gesture: Being the Abhinaya Darpana of Nandikesvara.* Harvard University Press.

2. Sharma, S. (2024). *Weaving 'delusional' stories: Case studies exploring the ontological aspects of delusional symptoms* [Unpublished manuscript]. School of Human Studies, Dr. B.R. Ambedkar University Delhi.

Chapter Thirteen
The 'other'

The "other," also called "the small other" in the Lacanian Lexicon; a relation with which is situated in the *Imaginary Order*. "But what relevance does it hold for the *Eye Ego*, let alone *Rasa*?" the reader may wonder. For that, let me explicitly add the word "eye" to Jacques Lacan's *Mirror Stage*, so the uncertainty the reader may have about my route of choice dissipates a little.

Lacan claims that when a child 'sees' their mirror reflection, they, for the first time, experience themselves as "whole".[1] At its core, identification with this mirror image is a projection and reflection of one's own ego. At the same time, the mirror reflection that the child sees comes to represent an idealized version of the child's self, due to it being seemingly cohesive. This "Ideal Ego" is the first introduction to the "other," also called the "small other." Seeing the mirror reflection is the first encounter with the "small other." While growing up, as the child interacts with other people, relationships with them too are formed on the same scheme. Siblings, friends, and adults are seen as mirrors that reflect back aspects of the child's own ego, as they are treated with projection and identification. Relationships with people are situated in the *Imaginary Order*, where the focus is on images (vision) and identifications, not language and social order (as these are elements of the *Symbolic Realm* — the big 'Other').

One navigates interpersonal relationships using the foundational schema formed through identification with their mirror reflection, a process facilitated by the eyes. Any interaction with another person primarily occurs through the script of one's own ego. This resonates with how an audience establishes a connection with an artist during a performance. In both, specialized performances and general life, interactions are dominated by imagination, identification, and fantasies—creations of the self. While the *Symbolic Order* mediates social interactions through language and law, performative arts, especially Indian classical dance, transcend the need for language by relying on bodily movements. Though drama employs language, it still recognizes the potency of bodily expressions to communicate with the audience. The invocation of *Rasa* in these performances does not require the intervention of the 'Other'; instead, it is a co-creation of the egos engaged in the creation and observation of the art. For instance, the earlier described *Akasa & Ullokita* eye glances, whose resonance with a clinical condition, are not bound by the *Symbolic Order* but are purely personal. Another example may be the tragic scene of Rama being desperate and sorrowful for not finding Sita at the hut upon returning having chased the golden deer. The audience, in moments like these, is able to empathetically feel what Ram feels even in a lack of verbal delivery from the artist. In Hindi, this resonance that happens in the audience for the character's internal state is called आत्मसाध: to make something one's own. This falls

congruent with the feature of *Identification*[2] that the ego adopts to navigate the 'other.'

This function of two people communicating their internal state without having to borrow language (an element of the big 'Other') is perhaps the purest form of connection that people can establish among themselves. The theory of *Rasa* in specific and human interactions in general, are founded on the ego's feature of identification and projection—just as with the image in the mirror. It is not just *Rasa*, the inception of which—through 'seeing' the performer's bodily gestures—is made possible by the ego's identification and projection mechanism, but also the faculty of empathy itself. As learned earlier, it is the eye that is at the core of both communicative exchanges (right since infancy) and the observation of one's own mirror reflection. So, I claim that empathy as a psychic function is a feature of the *Eye Ego*. The eye, as the physiological foundation for both the *Mirror Stage* and the genesis of the 'self,' is what later enables navigation of the 'other' and the ability to empathize with people—'others.'

The *Eye Ego,* with its ability to facilitate dialectical relations with others, not only gives scope to understand art and experience Rasa but also any form of relation with people.

"एक प्यार का नगमा है

मौजों की रवानी है

एक प्यार का नगमा है

मौजों की रवानी है

ज़िंदगी और कुछ भी नहीं

तेरी मेरी कहानी है"

~ Santosh Anand

Perhaps these lyrics, sung by Mukesh and Lata, come closest to my otherwise intellectual speculation: "Life is nothing but a co-created narrative of the egos".

Though for the sake of it, multiple sources that suggest that "the experience of 'self' comes to be only in relation to others", could be referred to at this site. But it would be wiser to leave my proposition at this moment and have faith in the reader's विवेक and let them test these thoughts of mine for themself.

References

1. Lacan, J. (1949). The mirror stage as formative of the function of the I as revealed in psychoanalytic experience. In *Écrits: A Selection* (A. Sheridan, Trans., 1977). W. W. Norton & Company.

2. ibid

Chapter Fourteen
The 'Other'

In the previous section, we talked about the role of the Eye Ego in establishing a dialectical relation that helps navigate the 'other.' In this section, we will explore the essential yet unacknowledged contribution of the Eye Ego in accessing the *Symbolic Order.*

We can think of navigating the 'other' as a lateral relation to the world around us, as the 'other'—situated in the *Imaginary Order*—constitutes things dealt with through identification and imagination. Think of it as points on a paper connected by singular paths. The ego, like a point in space, can navigate the 'other' only to the extent that projection and identification allow in the absence of a broader dimension. However, life's navigation requires more than the ego's mechanisms of projection and identification. There is another order, beyond the *Imaginary*, called the *Symbolic Order*, also known as the "big Other."

For those unfamiliar with this Lacanian concept, think of the *Symbolic Order* as the social context in which a person exists—social groups, families, laws, morality, and most prominently, language; it as the context in which a person exists. This could be their social group, family, law, morality and most popularly in the the discourse of Lacan, the 'language'.

In this chapter, I posit in succession to my proposition on how it is the Eye Ego, which is at the core of ego dialectics, that gives rise to human relations and co-created experiences; now I aim to explore the role of the Eye Ego—the psychic entity stemming from the physiological function of 'seeing'—in 'enabling' navigation of the 'Other'. I consider it essential to explicitly state to the reader that, what I propose here is not a psychic feature that in itself lets the individual access the Symbolic Order but rather what enables the ability to access it. This section traces the Eye Ego in developments that happened prior to the introduction of the Symbolic Order but still are essential for its access.

The kernel for these interpersonal relations is designed through early intellectual experiences, prominently the mirror stage.

Each sense organ works as a window to the world—the interaction with which was the primary cause for the ego's genesis. Each sensation, with its distinct quality, is at the core of our experience of the world; while not just an outward orientation to the world, they make their place in our psyche as active agents of arranging experiences. By this, I mean that the quality or, to say, the 'method' of experiencing the world is adopted by the way sensory organs function. It is in Lacan's *Mirror*

Stage that the child is introduced to their mirror reflection, making them familiar with the concept of *symbolisation*[1]—one thing can represent something that it itself is not—just as the 'self' is presented to the world in the shape of the child's appearance even though it is not their experience of their self. *Alienation* experienced by the child creates a gap in him between his inner experience of oneself and how he is experienced by the world—one's external appearance. Here, the child, for the first time, learns that he is a separate subject capable of interacting with the world. Though Lacan misses this, it is essentially the eye that enables the aspect of symbolisation, which, in its advanced form, develops the faculty of language. So, if the reader is aware of the Lacanian lexicon, I state that the eye—precisely the act of seeing—among other things—is at the core of a person accessing the *Other*.

In my observation, I have found two stages of development that enable the access of the 'Other', where the Eye Ego plays a key role with its ability to subject and be subjected. I am certain that psychic developments never cease to persist, but I have found two very important stages that kick-start for a child, the development of the essential tools—presumably the ego—to access the Other. I do not intend to give the reader an idea that this 'Other' is a distant form of reality of being that requires a frame of thought of an extraordinary kind. The tools we use to navigate this realm become an inseparable part of our self, so much so that the idea of identifying them itself may seem idiotic. We individuals have been inhabiting this Symbolic realm right since, or even before our birth. This reminds me of what Heidegger calls "thrownness".[2] People do not choose to be born in the conditions that they find themselves in, which perhaps is one of the tragedies of life. It is this 'context' that brings the dots discussed earlier, a third dimension to connect from.

The first introduction of a person to the 'Other' happens during infancy. During this early phase of life, the 'Other' is embodied by the mother, and it is from this Other, that the child acquires language, social laws and the rough map for life navigation.[3] According to Lacan, this transmission of the Other from the mother, is the primary identification that one goes through. I say, it is not just an exposure to the Other that comes through the mother, but the design of the psyche, especially the ego. Tracing the possible inheritance of the ego from the mother is a matter in itself, and requires exclusive attention in order to be developed further.[§§] So, here I limit myself solely to the inspection of the Other through the mother.

The second instance that comes as a milestone on the way of gaining access to the Other is the

---

§§ *Ego Architecture*

Mirror Stage. The learning that one thing can represent something that it itself is not, comes for the first time in the mirror stage. *Alienation* and *Symbolisation,* at this stage, enable one to later develop language by the creation of a 'small other' to which signifiers attach. A child who does not go through the essential phase of alienation may never even develop the ability to understand language as he has no access to the Other.[4] I am not sure about the literal validity of the previous statement, but the idea that people who find it difficult to understand metaphors (using words to signify something other than their literal meaning) indicates that perhaps there is some truth to the above-mentioned claim by Lacan.

The importance of the Mirror Stage and the mother as the first Other have received adequate attention and refinement to their theoretical construction in regard to how they facilitate access to the Other. I do not intend to restate Lacan's thoughts as if he failed to do it for himself. I understand that doing this would greatly benefit a lesser-known thinker, but I do not wish to stress the reader by presenting them with a lengthy text to wrestle with. Here, I seek to trace the Eye Ego in existing theory and build a solid foundation for it to later someday build a full-fledged system on it.

Lacan, states that in the process of acquiring 'language' from the mother, the child also acquires the entire 'Other' of the mother, namely her attitudes, rules, assumptions, etc.[5] This 'Other' serves as the context within which one lives their life. It is not just genes and nurturance that parents become the source of, but the very context of life. In India, certainly for the right reasons, the mother has been designated as पहली गुरु—the first teacher.

The mother, in teaching language to her child, passes a key to him to navigate the world. Here, I find scope for an exploration of how "intergenerational trauma" is passed from one generation to another. There must be a tint in the parents' vocabulary that the child picks up, which perhaps becomes one of the carriers of the parents' sorrows and life experiences. The speculation made in the chapter 'Love' suggests that the foundation for the interpersonal dialectics between people that serve as the pathway for ideas, mutual experiences, and empathy is laid early in infancy between the mother and infant. In popular clinical literature and diagnostic style, a resemblance of any psychological symptoms among family members is quickly deduced as "a hereditary illness". I think blaming biology or genetic predisposition for a psychic condition that multiple members of a family suffer from is the easiest and slackest thing to do. There could be innumerable ways of tracing this 'transfer' between the parents and the child, but the parents' 'Other', inherited by the child, is plausibly one of the most convincing pathways that can bring some clarity on the matter of how certain psychopathologies travel from one person to another. Lacan, in one of his early works, *Family Complexes*, addresses how the child's identification with the parents and their desires, can lead to psychopathology.[6] What I am suggesting is that the process of learning a language and sharing a constant dialectical relation with the parents (or other family members) can make the child inherit the parent's faulty relations with the Other. Depression and OCD are perhaps the most common psychopathologies, both of which are born out of problematic relations with the Other. Sharing space with an obsessive parent, especially when the parent is the source of the 'Other' in the child's life, could be one of the major reasons why such illnesses are likely to be found in multiple members of a family if found in one.[***]

In Lacanian literature, it is the mirror stage that is the first leap towards the access of the Other. The idea of 'self', which is created by 'seeing' the mirror reflection, is what 'signifiers' attach to. According to Lacan, it is this stage that enables the acquisition of language and, in turn, access to the Other. But I say that the idea of 'self' is not a creation of the mirror stage but of the mother's gaze upon the baby. The idea of 'self', which according to Lacan, is created when the baby 'sees' himself, actually predates the baby's 'seeing'. The 'self' is induced by the mother's action of 'seeing'

[***] *Psychic Architecture: Ego Architecture*

the baby, and what happens during the mirror stage, is that the baby 'sees' what the mother and other adults have been 'seeing' when addressing the baby. Just as the idea of 'self' existed before the mirror stage, so did the attachment of signifiers to it. What has conventionally been thought a leap towards access to the Other might actually be a development of a pre-existing psychic feature—the Eye Ego. In either case—of when does the idea of 'self' come to be—it is the Eye Ego's function to witness the world and enable the concept of *Symbolisation.*

*

References

1. Lacan, J. (1949). The mirror stage as formative of the function of the I as revealed in psychoanalytic experience. In *Écrits: A Selection* (A. Sheridan, Trans., 1977). W. W. Norton & Company.

2. Heidegger, M. (1927). *Being and Time.* Harper & Row.

3. Lacan, J. (1978). *The four fundamental concepts of psychoanalysis* (A. Sheridan, Trans.). W.W. Norton & Company. (Original work published 1964).

4. ibid

5. ibid

6. Lacan, J. (1938). Les complexes familiaux. In *Encyclopédie française* (Vol. 8). Paris.

Chapter Fifteen

Evil Eye

In Indian culture, there is a long-running tradition of mothers putting *kajal* around the contours of their babies' eyes, with the intention to protect the baby from *nazar*, which young ones are believed to be especially vulnerable to. In case somebody's evil eye affects the baby, the baby is under the threat of suffering physical illness alongside psychological suffering. *Kajal* comes as a rescue to the weak defenses of the young baby's Eye Ego, which is not yet strong enough to fight the psychological hostility from the outside world. Freud considered the fear of the evil eye to be born out of one's own projections.[1] In the case of adults, the fear of the evil eye is believed to originate in person A from projected feelings of jealousy onto person B. These projected feelings are what person A would feel in regard to themselves if they were in person B's position. But children being vulnerable to the evil eye indicates that there might be some truth to the fear of it.

However, the supposed efficiency of its 'cure' for children and even infants tells us that it cannot be dismissed by being called a neurotic symptom. Even if it were just a neurotic fear, its presence in infants requires a fresh perspective on the phenomenon. The strongest indicator towards the possibility of it being more than neurosis is the efficiency of curative measures that produce satisfactory results for children. Of course, I am considering the rituals and the protective measures as efficient by seeing their prevalence and leaving the job for a quantitative study to the research psychology folks who have not made it this far into the text.

As stated earlier, the interpersonal dialectic between egos becomes possible, credited to the pathway of the Eye Ego. The ritual of putting a physical barrier on the eye contours is a manifestation of a subtle belief that psychological hostility 'enters' the eyes through another person's gaze, and primarily affects the 'self' residing behind the eyes. The act of putting a काला टीका—a black dot— either on the forehead or elsewhere on the body in a concealed manner is done with the intention of giving the baby a third eye. This ritual of giving the baby a third eye presumably stems from a belief that it is the eyes that are responsible for defending the 'self'. For the child, the experience of getting a dot drawn on his body by the mother must be that of "receiving an eye from the parent (which is always the mother) which would protect me from harm". This assurance of psychic protection by the mother is an alive desire of the Hindu psyche. Just as the baby once felt protected in the mother's गोदी, later, he does so with the *maternal eye* on his body. The aliveness of this desire to be under the mother's protection even in adulthood gets expressed in Hindu prayers of both men and women asking देवी माँ to protect their bodies, wealth, prestige and loved ones. मार्कंडेय पुराण contains a hymn named दुर्गा रक्षा कवच, recitation of which is believed to ward off injuries and death. In the hymn, different forms of the divine mother are being asked to protect different body parts, like arms, spine, torso, etc. The popular belief is that its recitation protects one from negative energies and misfortune—which may be synonymous with psychic fears.

In the Mahabharata, right before the 18th day of the battle, there is a description of a significant exchange between Duryodhana and his mother, Gandhari. Gandhari, after her marriage to Dhritarashtra (who was blind since birth), decides to remain blindfolded for the rest of her life so she could share her husband's experience of blindness. After the battle on the 17th day, when Duryodhana's defeat was certain, as with the death of most of his brothers and Karna, it was known that the 18th day would be conclusive for the war. Gandhari, worried for Duryodhana's life, decides to remove her blindfold and bless her son with her 'vision', hoping this would protect him. Duryodhana, upon Krishna's suggestion, decided to cover his groin, as it was only modest to not appear naked in front of one's mother. A fear in the Pandva's camp on the possibility of Duryodhana becoming immune to any injury by his mother's blessings, indicates a hint of reality in the belief that the *mother's eye*, indeed, is protective of the child. The 'mistake' of not appearing naked in front of his mother, costs Duryodhana his life, as his thighs had not been under his mother's *gaze*.

Just like the *maternal eye*, there is a *paternal eye—Shiv's third eye*. The figure of Shiva is housed in the Hindu psyche as the paternal figure. Alongside his simple and easy-to-please form भोलेनाथ, नीलकंठ: the one to drank poison on others' behalf, he is also known for his fierce form, रुद्र. Just like the father, he resides in the Hindu psyche in an intimate and feared form. What is of interest here is his angry form, where he is believed to have all his three eyes open—त्रिनेत्र or त्रिलोचन. This angry form of his—though rare—is believed to bring *transformation, order* and *death to desires*. To attain its 'transformative' aims, the world (synonymous with the 'psyche') has to go through a phase of destruction. This *paternal eye*, in compliment to the *maternal eye*, is a resident of the Hindu mind. The mother, with her protective and nurturing qualities, gives the child her 'eye' to rescue him from threats of injury or death, whereas the father, with his harsh nature, brings order to life, takes threats & pains onto himself, and seeks to bring transformation. These "psychic eyes", are perhaps interjections from the parents. During the process of nurturance, both the parents, with their distinct qualities and roles, come to be situated in the child's mind, and the child uses aspects of the parent's egos to navigate his life.

Given my findings and formulations until now, I have enough reasons to conclude that the Evil Eye is a poorly articulated intellectual construct built on the feeling of envy or hostility that a person unconsciously senses in others in regard to themself. The undercurrent communication that people engage in, becomes a mode of communicating hostilities and psychic violence, the feeling of "being affected by which" is expressed in experiencing poor health—the origins for which are psychosomatic. The Eye Ego is the defensive front against intrapersonal hostility and envy for oneself, that may be sensed in others. Protection against the evil eye comes from maternal gestures, which continue to reside in the psyche probably for the entire life to come.

*

References

1. Freud, S. (1919). The uncanny. In J. Strachey (Ed. & Trans.), The standard edition of the complete psychological works of Sigmund Freud (Vol. 17, pp. 217-256). Hogarth Press.

Chapter Sixteen
Self-Permanence

It is a commonly seen phenomenon among children to close their eyes while playing, with the intention "If I close my eyes, I shall become invisible to others". Children resort to closing their eyes, as an attempt to cease existing to the outside world. To me, it is intriguing how the simple idea of "disappearance" is played out by children in the most nonchalant way. Imagine an adult thinking to themself, "If only I close my eyes, I shall be spared of these current circumstances". The reader—if informed about psychopathology—is bound to consider a potential statement like this by an adult as a matter of concern. But what if I say that infantile beliefs like this are very much active components of what we understand as the adults' psyche?

It is not rare among children to resort to closing their eyes during the play of 'Hide-and-seek', with the intention that if they happen to close their eyes, they would disappear from the outer world. Just like any mental belief or pattern, this has a cause behind its existence—that too is a very prominent one. If it were to be seen in light of my previous propositions on the roles of the *Eye Ego,* this infantile phenomenon would reveal its deep undercurrents—that may even inform us about the architecture of the psyche. In the previous section, it was established that *vision* has an important role to play in the development of the 'self'. The experience of 'seeing' oneself was found to be of immense importance in the creation of the self, but inspecting this infantile belief, we learn that the development of a 'self' on the grounds of visual information of one's body is not a one-time thing—never requiring revision. It rather, is a momentary phenomenon. The self has to be synthesised each moment. But I still do not think that eyes alone carry out this task, but the experience they produce, certainly is the most dominant in the psychic narrative of the 'self'.

But before we proceed with examining this rather bizarre infantile belief, let us trace the same in adult psychic life.

There is no convincing answer, if any, to this widely observed phenomenon among children. The dominant narrative in Psychology may dismiss this as a result of poor cognitive skills, but it still would not do justice to the "how" of the matter. While I believe, my stance on this might be clear to the reader, that children resort to closing their eyes because of their belief that if they cannot see themself, they do not exist.

I cannot see myself, therefore I am not.

But still, I believe greater clarity awaits us if we refer to the available theories from *Developmental*

Literature—that track the development of the ego from a different perspective. According to the *Theory of Mind,* due to the limited cognitive ability among children to understand perspectives that are different from theirs, they lack the ability to fathom anything that is not in their sensory experiences. Classic experiments like the *Blanket and Ball Study*[1] and *Three Mountain Task,*[2] through the concept of *Object Permeance* and *Perspectiveism,* respectively, demonstrate that children (up until a certain age) fail to understand the world outside their immediate sensory experience—specifically their visual perception. The inability to understand the world away from the sensory experiences of oneself has been a widely recognised phenomenon—credited to *ego-centrism.*[3]

I propose that this rather unintelligent act of closing one's eyes informs us about the possibility that a child believes themself to exist just because they 'see' themself. The belief that others would not be able to see them if they closed their eyes implies their opinion that the child believes that "I exist because I can see myself", and not the other way that "I exist, therefore I can see myself". Now, one may argue that what is being intended in moments of 'closed eyes' is just a disappearance and not a 'cease' in being. This is answered by referring to another *egocentric* phenomenon, of *Object Permanence:* objects cease to exist when they are out of sight. This 'out of sight-ness' is replicated in moments of closed eyes—during play—with the intention of 'not existing'. My claim that "the eyes play a crucial role in maintaining the permanence of the self" is also supplemented by *Jacques Lacan's Mirror Stage,* where the child, for the first time, experiences himself as a unified entity after 'seeing' oneself in the mirror.

Developmental theories consider this as an impermanent state of development, which is meant to be grown out of, but even the most casual knower of Psychoanalysis would know that it is not the case. Infantile beliefs and complexes are permanent residents of the human psyche, unaffected by the scrutiny of time. They are deposited in the archaic layers of the psyche, influencing one's life. I engage with the 'aliveness' of these rather unintelligent beliefs in the next section, where I transcend the boundaries of the body to trace the ego.

For now, at the core of my claim is that the eyes play a very important role in establishing the *self* (and its permanence). The *Eye Ego* renders the cloud of sensations—the body—into a unified entity. The skin *holds*, and the eye *acknowledges.*

References

1. Piaget, J. (1955). The development of object permanence. In *The construction of reality in the child* (pp. 3-96). Basic Books.

2. Piaget, J., & Inhelder, B. (1956). *The child's conception of space*. Routledge & Kegan Paul.

3. Flavell, J. H. (1992). Cognitive development: Past, present, and future. *Developmental Psychology, 28*(6), 998–1005. https://doi.org/10.1037/0012-1649.28.6.998

Section C: Beyond the Body

Chapter Sixteen
Beyond the Cartesian Model

Shadow, "Aah, the Shadow!". It was one of the initial insights that put me on this path, which I believe I would not abandon if I choose to stick to the discipline of Psychology further in my life. I have thoughtfully placed the chapter before what is to follow. Perhaps it would be easier to transition from the known plain of Psychology—the body, to elsewhere—the place I have not named yet. Let me begin the chapter by making the reader recall a riddle they must have heard before. What is the size of an elephant but is lighter than air?

The shadow is like the nose, always in view but never in perception. Due to its immateriality in both bodily functions and (supposed) psychological insignificance, the shadow has not received its due recognition. Psychology, with its aspiration to be scientific and being coupled with human sciences, begins and ends around the human body. Well, you may think, "What else is there to being human other than the body?". In this final section of the book, *Beyond the Body* is what I aim to explore. For this pursuit of mine, I am choosing the *shadow* as the connecting link between the body and what I would eventually attempt to give the reader a glimpse of.

Writing this section poses a unique challenge to me, as there seem to be no apparent entry points for me to dive into this matter. The idea of introducing such aspects to Psychology itself may seem bizarre and uncalled for, for there is no apparent utility for things like these. I respect such doubts and take it as a task to convince the reader about the psychological significance of the shadow.

Spiritual-to-material has been a rather dramatic shift in the recent history of humans. Speculations about the nature of existence, the human condition, and orientation towards life have made a significant positional shift both in academia and in general human temperament. Where mysticism was an accepted tradition of thought that allowed speculations to be born in the absence of empirical traces, with Western enlightenment, there was an appreciation for scientific temperament and the production of results that could be verified on a variety of aspects. No matter what and how we (the children of science) advocate for the precision of scientific pursuits and its tolerance for results and opinions, at the core of scientific *verificationism* stays the satiation of our senses. Scientific disciplines demand their results and answers to be visible to the human eye, almost to be tactile in their feature and communicable in their nature. The greatest beating for this reason took the religions all over the world. While with an understating of science came an ability to command nature, it also threatened the civilisational values that served as the core of being. I want the reader to know that I believe that religion is not just a fungus that develops in the absence of light (science), but it is the medicine for the human fever. Religion and spirituality serve answers that are visceral and satisfying. Therefore, their speculations cannot be replaced by thoughts and sequence of logic (as science attempts to do). Mine is an attempt to provide a अध्यतामिक (spiritual) answer to the अध्यतामिक hunger. My appeal is not to deem ourselves as satiated by stuffing ourselves with the feed that is not meant for us.

Chapter Eighteen
Double

The idea of a 'double' self has been a resident of horror stories and fantasies for time immemorial. Fictitious themes like that of doppelgangers, ghosts, and souls, are known for the uncanniness that they can produce in the audience. A psychoanalytically significant legend that has been widely recognized for its theme of 'two' is that of Narcissus. Narcissus was a young man who, upon seeing his reflection in the water, could not take his eye off and eventually died. While popularly, we understand that Narcissus fell in love with himself, but it is the occasion and the medium that is important. We understand from the myth, the tendency among humans to fall in love with their own self, which is now called *Narcissism*. What we miss here is the 'medium' that made Narcissus not move, and eventually die. Freud understood this myth as a literary demonstration of how people develop an excessive self-love that, at times, takes the shape of psychopathology. Let's keep Freud's understanding of *narcissism* aside for now, and visit the myth afresh.

The young man had been living an adventurous life full of hunting, passion, and prestige. As a possessor of extraordinary beauty and exceptional hunting skills, he had plenty to be proud of. Then, one day, upon seeing his reflection in a pool, he fell in love with the image. I say that he chose not to move, not because he wanted to keep looking at himself in the water, but to avoid making the reflection disappear. In the moment of 'seeing,' it was not his 'self' that he fell in love with, but the image. He had been living a rather rich life until then, which would not have been possible without healthy ego functions. Though reserved in his personality, according to one version of the myth, he had a younger sister whom he loved dearly. Inspecting his life, I find no reason to speculate that he had any narcissistic tendencies. But, having received a curse of falling in love with himself, he became transfixed by his image and eventually died. We have been mistaking his love for the reflection—his 'double', for his love for himself. Had it been an intense love for himself, he would have chosen survival, over transfixion. In that life-ending instance, his only objective was to ensure the sustenance of the reflection, which he indeed fulfilled till the end.

The 'doubles' like reflections, shadows and ghosts, become gateways to the other side of the psyche that cannot be traced by popular psychology or perhaps even by psychoanalysis of the rudimentary kind. The myth of Narcissus communicates the psychological significance of the 'double' or the 'other'. Still, this 'other' is a direct manifestation of the body. I would like to point out that his 'other' is not to be confused with the Lacanian 'other'. At times, I would refrain from the use of the term "psychological" alongside "significance", as I believe that the topics that would be explored, cannot be exhausted under the lens of Psychology alone.

There is a variety of attempts that humans make to cope with the fear of death, one of these being writing a book—as chosen by yours truly. The one that holds significance for our enquiry of the 'double', is the idea of *ghosts.* The idea that a 'self' can wander the world even after the body has died is a prominent fantasy. In the initial investigation of the fear of ghosts among various cultures and religions, one may conclude it is a fear of the human mind that is present cross-culturally. But actually, the belief that people become ghosts after death is a fantasy disguised as fear. Sticking to the popular understanding of ego genesis—the body being the site where the ego originates, we learnt about the psychological significance of the body and corporeality of the ego. Dealing with the fear of death of the body, becomes a task for the ego; alongside the death of the body, the death of the ego itself becomes a matter of concern. Death, with its inevitability, is dealt with, by knitting the fiction of ghosts and spirits—egos that are independent of any 'bodies'. A 'spirit' is thought of as a core element of a person that can exist independently of the body. So, a 'ghost' is nothing but an ego without the body. 'Fictions' like these do not remain limited to the thought apparatus, but become elements of culture, collective psyche and language. So, more than a personal defence curated by the ego, belief in ghosts and life after death is a culturally sanctioned rescue.

Carrying forward the propositions made in the chapters related to *The Eye Ego* (particularly in *Love* and *The Other*), it is the correspondence between the mother and the baby that serves as the foundation for any interpersonal relations and the child's introduction into the social order. I also proposed how the parents become the source of psychopathology in the child. While aspects like "pathologies" are clinically observable, they are not all that is inherited from the parents or the greater context—society. In the chapter *Love*, I made a passing remark about the possibility that our entire psychic structure or organization is built on introjections from the outside.[†††] This might be the reason why there are distinctions between the psyches of people from different cultures. "Why do you recall that here?" you may wonder. Well, concepts like that of 'ghosts' in "primitive" cultures and the idea that human consciousness could be downloaded into a hard drive in societies where God is dead are essentially cultural defenses against the fear of death. In either case, the fantasy of being able to transcend death even after the

---

[†††] *Ego Architecture*

destruction of the body demands the creation of a 'self' independent of the body. The reason for me recalling the previously built idea that "the psychic structure is inherited" paves the way to situate the possibility that cultural ideas like 'ghosts' are 'learned' by the individual, which make active functional shifts in the personal psyche. By "functional" I mean living with the provision of a 'self' independent of the body. Such defenses do not remain personal affairs but become collective knowledge. The idea that the psychic organization, or the ego structure, is a collective construct is demonstrated by the palpable fear of ghosts. No matter how much a person tries to logically cut through these beliefs, the visceral reality—the chills and the goosebumps—do not cease to be. This tells that belief in a 'self' independent of the body is not a matter of personal opinions that could be discarded with reason; rather, this is a 'given' for which the psyche has to make an accommodation.

Chapter Nineteen
Shadow Defense

The arguments in favour of the shadow being an element of the ego, by virtue of being a medium of expression and the supposed loss of it being a psychic fear, do not by themself establish the shadow as a facilitator or an element of the ego; but it has certainly got our foot in the door. This 2-dimensional self, that at all times accompanies the individual, is the aspect of the 'self' in a different physical and psychic dimension. It would be futile to describe the psychical aspect of this 'self'. As mentioned before, the ego, in order to defend itself against the fear of death, develops 'doubles' of itself. These 'doubles' are not spare bodies, but dynamic entities with lives of their own. Ofcourse, it would be needless to say that it is from the personal psyche that the inanimate shadow or the fiction of spirits are given life, but it is to the credit of these 'doubles', that unique aspects of the ego—that could not have developed, or would not have been active in the body alone—are given life. It is this dimension of the psyche that I aim to explore in this final section of the book.

The 'doubles', whose aim is to rescue the ego from the fear of annihilation of the body, become characters of the psychic life—graduating from begin insurance against death to being aspects of the ego that are crucial for a variety of psychic functions. Freud states something similar in his essay *The Uncanny*.[1]

"Such ideas, however, have sprung from the soil of unbounded self-love, from the primary narcissism which holds sway in the mind of the child as in that of primitive man; and when this stage has been left behind the double takes on a different aspect. From having been an assurance of immortality, he becomes the ghastly harbinger of death."

~ Freud, 1919

The dimension of the psychic life I refer here, is intimately related to the world of ghosts, spirits and black magic. Discussing *The Evil Eye* in the previous section, I indicated towards the possibility of a greater force active in the phenomenon than just neuroticism. This other dimension facilitates an interaction between the 'doubles' of different people. I am shying away from calling it the "unconscious", as what is to follow would not necessarily comply with our popular understanding of it. Even if this 'dimension' could be accommodated in the existing knowledge of the 'unconscious', it would happen on the extreme most stretch of it. Consider this dimension, as a plain beyond comprehension, which can only be assumed about by observing changes in the plain visible to us. It is a battleground of some other world, and we can only assume its dynamics by observing the effects it has on our world. The reason why I call it a "battleground" is that it constitutes hostile exchanges between egos. The other reason for it being called a "battleground" is that, for now, I have been able to understand it only for hostile exchanges and the defences employed by the egos for their 'protection'. If in future I revisit these ideas, I may switch the term for something else.

Carl Jung, in his essay, *The Basic Postulates of Analytical Psychology*,[2] while explaining various ancient views on the 'Soul', captures several essential aspects of the psyche, which, according to various civilizations, were the sources of life. He writes,

> *"Very often the soul is also identified with the shadow, hence it is a deadly insult to tread on a person's shadow. For the same reason noonday, the ghost-hour of southern latitudes, is considered threatening; one's shadow then grows small, and this means that life is endangered. This conception of the shadow contains an idea which was indicated by the Greeks in the word 'synopados', "he who follows behind'."*

~ Jung 1933

The shadow—an insurance against death, is created through the mediation of the self and the world. It, in other terms, is proof of one's existence.

The fictitious theme of losing one's shadow, seeks to invoke the fear of death in the audience through the mechanism of depriving the character of the evidence of their existence in the other realm—the culturally curated realm of spirits and ghosts. The Indian ghostly figure, called भूत, is traditionally believed to be an entity that comes into existence after an untimely or painful death of a person. The भूत visually resembles the bodily form of the person from which it originated and wonders the world, seeking a 'body' to attain liberation. The figure of भूत is firmly housed in the Indian psyche. Often choosing to stay alone, they seldom 'capture' a human, and make their body a vehicle to fulfill their desires. Like any other psychological phenomenon, the period of childhood, here too, is a site for fertile observations. Usually, the fear of भूत is acquired during childhood, evidently due to the relatively weak ego structure at this stage. The figure of भूत is introduced as an entity that seeks to cause harm—an entity that is hostile to the ego. There are cultural remedies like *sacred threads, ash* and *Talisman,* that are hung on the body to guard oneself against any ghostly figures. I am not sure if the reader is aware of the precautionary measures taken by some people—at least in North India—to avoid leaving home around noon. Another such advisory is to avoid haunted places and pathways after sunset. Both these prescriptions are to be followed, even secretly, if one intends to go anywhere near a cremation ground or a site infamous for ghost sightings. The fear of ghosts is even greater during the night of अमावस्या—the moonless night. The aspect common among situations like noontime, with the sun positioned exactly above the head and at night especially if it अमावस्या, is that a person forms no shadow.

We fear encountering ghosts after sunset because there is no shadow accompanying us at that time.

A person is valuable to a ghost, as they have something that the wondering ego lacks— a body. I must remind the reader at this point, that the ego is essentially a bodily entity, which ghosts lack. This 'lack' helps us understand the longing that ghosts are believed to be stuck in. The figure of a ghost is representative of an incomplete psyche. I might divert from the primary topic, but I believe this discovery that a ghost is in a 'lack', opens venues for further explorations. A ghost is a feared state of being that occurs after death. It, essentially, is an entity that is in need of psychic harmony, which is a must for an incomplete psychic entity to attain liberation. A person is believed to likely turn into a ghost and remain wondering if there is an unfulfilled wish or a strong affective state like rage which must be resolved. So essentially, a ghost is a representation of a dissatisfied ego that needs to attain its objectives. It is a psychic construct that might occur within the personal psyche of a living person when one loses interest in the body and the social order. I speculate that the superego is lost when the body dies—as the individual can no longer be subjected to society's gaze and floats outside the social periphery away from constant revisions of social morality. Adjoining to this, we learn that the shadow is the defence of the body-ego. This explains why the thought (primarily explored only in fiction) of losing one's shadow invokes restlessness and fear—as one is afraid of either becoming or being captured by a ghost.

The vulnerability of encountering ghosts has to do with the cultural architecture of the 'ego'. The Hindu ego blueprint has provisions for psychic dimensions that extend beyond the personal unconscious. The relief (or burden) that comes with the belief that one would continue to exist as a soul even after the body dies, is accompanied by the creation of a space in the personal psyche to accommodate the parallel world of 'ghosts'—a construct of the collective psyche. Think of it as a cultural insurance against death that needs a subscription from the person at the cost of lending their personal psyche to the collectively curated world of ghosts.

References

1. Freud, S. (1919). *The uncanny.* In *The Standard Edition of the Complete Psychological Works of Sigmund Freud* (Vol. 17, pp. 217-256). Hogarth Press.

2. Jung, C. G. (1933). *The basic postulates of analytical psychology.* In W. S. Dell & C. F. Baynes (Trans.), *Modern man in search of a soul* (pp. 1-20). Harcourt, Brace & Company.

Chapter Twenty

Beyond the Body

Introduction

The various perspectives through which we have explored the ego so far have treated the 'body' as the ultimate truth. Whether that be the dynamics of the ego in meditative states, the *Skin Ego* or the *Eye Ego*, it is the body that serves as the kernel for the ego. Even the outlying concept of the *Shadow* as an aspect of the ego, sprouts out of the body—through physical interaction of the body and the world. The ego, as a psychic entity, exists to help the organism meet the demands of the world and ensure its survival, and I do not contest that.

What I do aim is to contest the dogma that the physical world is the only form of reality, that Psychology as a discipline should be concerned with. In the previous chapter, we exceed the physical 'self'—the body—to trace the ego. This breach may not be welcomed in academia, but I wish to surpass even the 'shadow'.

Kaliyuga

Sometime after the epic battle of *Mahabharata* ended, there existed a wise king, Parikshit. He, the grandson of Arjun and the son of Abhimanyu, was the ruler of the Kuru dynasty. One day while hunting, Parikshit encountered *Kali Purusha*—the embodied *Kali Yuga.* Kali requested the king to give him shelter in his kingdom, which Parikshit provided under some restrictions. Knowing the nature of Kali, he was allowed to reside in places associated with vise, such as gambling, drinking and brothels. Upon requesting, Kali was given one more place to reside in, gold. As time proceeded and the memory of the encounter faded, one day Parikshit discovered a beautiful gold throne in his storehouse, which he wore without thinking twice. This let Kali enter his mind and thus was the dawn of *Kali Yuga.* Changes in his personal demeanour after he wore the gold thrown were significant enough to attest that Kali had taken over his mind. Alongside this one incident, the entire society went through a tectonic shift. The era of Kali is believed to be associated with darkness and sins and is the last one of the four yugas. *Mahabharata* was written over 5,000 years ago; hence it has been this long since this yuga began.

Each yuga is considered more sinful than the previous one. With the battle of Mahabharat, violence had become the norm. A decline in morality had taken society by storm, and the residence of Kali on people's bodies in the form of gold came as the final straw, marking the beginning of the final yuga. Even though the yugas are periodical spans with definite lengths, their transitions are marked and traced primarily by shifts in social morality and human behaviour. This tells me that the primary value of this chronological system is to trace the shifts in the human mind, with each yuga being indicative of a collective psychic state of a particular kind.

What is so significant in the story of Parikshit is that he goes through a psychic shift after wearing a crown on his head. With the agreement, Kali was given an object of residence, which happened to be gold—a metal associated with social aspirations. Keeping in mind this story, we shall explore a novel aspect of the dynamic entity we call the 'ego': *Ego Objects.*

Psychic Life of Objects

The relationships one has with one's favourite clothes, jewellery, belongings, etc., are often taken for granted—a state that just happens to be—and are not recognized for the underlying script they are built on. The world, in its gross form, is an arrangement of the matter. Let us first discuss the experiential aspect of the relations one forms with objects before exploring the dynamic aspect of it. With "me", comes "mine". I say both "me" and "mine" are पुरक of each other. There can be no self

without objects to which 'it' clutches. Life is blown into an object for it to be accessed by the ego. The world of a child is the world of animism; the essence of any relations formed with worldly objects is this kernel of animism. *The phenomenon of animism is not a primitive, unintelligent form of seeing the world but a flavour of the 'self' experienced through the world.* The attribution of human-like qualities to the sky, trees, rivers, etc., comes from the tendency to project our own psychic contents onto the outer world. A relatively accepted childhood feature is to be of the opinion that all things around oneself a living beings. Jean Piaget considered animism as a stage of human cognition that is meant to be grown out of.[1] The animistic has the provision to accommodate not just the objects of the immediate environment, but even the planets and the stars. The belief that animism is a primitive form of looking at the world, which ceases to be once a higher form of cognition is attained, is not true. Animistic thought continues to reside in the unconscious, and does not fail to express itself in legends and poetry.

The understanding of 'ego', that we have abided by now, was useful for exploring aspects of the psyche—or psychology—that are concerned with the conventional subject matter that I call the "right hand" of psychology. For venturing into the "left hand" of psychology, we need to look at the ego from a perspective that is not bounded by the principles of the 'right side'. Ofcourse, I have adopted this distinction from the Hindu theology. दक्षिणाचार: the right-hand path that employs traditional means to reach god, whereas, वामाचार: the left-hand path makes use of rather shocking and socially unacceptable means to reach god. Both these paths are believed to lead the follower to the same destination but are polar opposites to each other. I find the same distinction valid in psychology, as what I am exploring does not fit popular psychological thought, and it could be quickly regarded as a study of neurotic beliefs rather than of the mind. The aspect of belief in spirits or animism is not a matter of intellectual agreement or disagreement. Animism could have been abandoned had it been socially constructed and propagated. Instead, it develops internally and is later furnished by cultural symbols. The prevalence of animism in cultures all over the world is evidence of some force at play that potentially exceeds our popular understanding of psychopathology. In psychology, animistic thinking is typically encountered in the context of psychopathology, such as in cases of OCD and schizophrenia. It is the nature of this encounter that has built our perspective of it as something that belongs to the world of the mad. Even if it is understood as something that is socially learnt, its importance in the psychic life of an individual has not become a subject of study. At best, psychology is tolerant of such 'illogical' aspects of the mind, which, if impossible to eliminate, should at least be kept in check. Animistic life is lived adjacent to the 'life' we know about, and both might be more intimate than we consider them to be. My invitation to the reader is to, for the span of some time, keep aside the terms like 'pathology', 'neuroticism', and 'psychosis' and see animism for what it appears to be.

Ego Objects

The body comes to be identified by the ego not just through the route of sensations, but also through its constant presence. The ego develops as a nucleus and later spreads to the body as one understands that it is the periphery called the 'skin' at which the self meets the world. The skin is undoubtedly the container of the ego, but there is more to it than just a place to be housed in—the body. Objects like clothes, glasses, and jewellery, to the credit of being in constant contact with the body, come to be devoured by the ego in seek of an extension of itself. "Certain elements of the body-ego may, through sensory contact with an object, undergo some degree of magnification."[2], writes Robert Fliss in *Ego and Body Ego*. Referring to Paul Schilder, he also claims that "body image" can extend to objects that are in direct contact to the body; Schilder also gives an example of a person holding a stick, in which case the stick becomes a part of his body due to the transfer of sensations from the stick to the hand of the person holding it.[3]

Just like previously explored aspects of the ego through cultural beliefs and myths, the belief that objects that come in direct contact with a person for a prolonged period of time come to carry the "energies" of the person is culturally sanctioned. I am not vouching for the credibility of these beliefs, and I am not referring to these cultural beliefs as evidence to prove my claims. Mine is a proposal that is in a nascent state, which I hope to build further in future. The merit in referring these cultural beliefs is that they enable us to trace those psychic developments and provisions that are facilitated by the individual's atmosphere. Just as the fear of being watched by god may become a source for psychopathology, or the belief in the afterlife may help a person deal with the loss of a loved one and fear of death; the opinion that one's "energies" continue to exist in objects one owns, facilitates a provision for a certain kind of structure of the ego that extends beyond the body.

The Sanskrit term *Runanubandha* is concerned *with the* 'energies' that one accumulates and leaves behind through physical contact one makes with people and objects. Samskaras, as impressions of past actions and experiences, are believed to be deposited in the psyche. The skin plays a crucial in the dynamics of *Runanubandha,* as it acts as a repository for it.[4] This is similar to the claims made by Anzieu in *The Skin Ego,* which indicates the possibility of some truth to these cultural beliefs. It is prescribed that as soon as a person dies, the cloths that have recently been in their physical contact should be burnt off, and their precious belongings should be distributed among multiple family members within the first three days. These measures are taken so the spirit gets confused and does not have a place to stick around in the absence of the body—which too has to be cremated as soon as possible.[5] The cultural fear behind these measures is that if these belongings are not dealt with appropriately, the dead person's spirit is likely to linger around.

Studying the 'shadow' was my first attempt to breach the 'soma', and its supposed hegemony in the psychological functions. The shadow acting as a defence against psychotic fears informs us about the variety of objects that the ego can employ to maintain its cohesion and psychic integrity. Objects that are possessed by the ego are cathexed with ego-libido, which makes them lively and active parts of our psychic life. While not just personal, these objects that come to supplement the ego could be culturally determined; for this, let us revisit the story of Parikshit. The choice of residence for Kali was gold; and for a significant period of time, the gold crown where he resided was left unnoticed, before it was worn by Parikshit one day, which let Kali take over the king's mind. In this story, the object (the crown) came to signify carrier of a psychic pathogen that attached itself to the king's ego. Another example of psychically significant objects would be religious threads, amulets and other such objects that are to be kept in contact to the body. In the case of these objects, the person who makes use of them usually seeks to protect themself from superstitious fears. "Superstitious fears" is just another term for fears whose origin is unknown. We previously learnt the importance of the shadow in guarding one against disembodied egos, but a defence like the shadow is of little value when the feared figure is of an origin that is not person-al. The figure of भूत, for instance,

a representation of a shattered psyche, shares the same kernel as an otherwise cohesive psyche—the ordinary mind; therefore, the defence constructed by the ego—the shadow—proves to be effective against it. But there exist such feared figures (psychotic fears) whose origin is not person-al, hence to defend oneself against them, the personal ego has to make use of 'objects' beyond itself. पिशाचा, for example, an entity created by Brahma,

which usually resides near a cremation ground, does not have its origin in an infantile fear or in the fear of death. Figures like these, with their vividly feared descriptions, do not have an origin in our personal psyches; rather, they are collectively constructed. In case of fears like this, the ego finds itself lacking any clue as to what to work with to defend oneself. To defend against figures like these, usually, the ego makes use of sacred threads and matras. Matra: a sound or a phrase that has to be repeated internally. The repetition of a mantra often takes a neurotic form; it is this obsession with the word or a sound that comes as a defence against the psychotic fear. Similarly, a sacred thread: an object that is to be made and distributed from a specific place—often a temple—comes as a rescue from fear. In both cases, a construct that is not personal, comes to assist the ego against psychosis. Whether that be the thread or the mantra, both come as additions to the ego. Only these defences that are shared collectively are effective against collective fears.

All this for the esoteric aspects of the human psyche. I would not want to supplement my claims of there being more to the script of the ego than just the body, merely by referring to the shared objects that come as reinforcements against symptoms of psychopathology. The other valid entry point into the matter that I have discovered is the tradition of hereditary objects. A cope against death, though not as 'quiet' as the shadow, is a baby of one's own. Now that I think about it, one tries to make their child a 'double' of theirs quite literally. Biologists would say that it is the genes that make people reproduce, but it is not just the biological blueprint that a child is made up of. The accumulations that one makes during their lifetime, at least in the Indian context, are motivated by the desire to create wealth for the generation to come. Objects that are cathexed by one's ego go on to exist long after the person has departed. Objects like jewellery, hats, watches, and tools of daily use, are often distributed among family members after the owner of the objects dies. An object that was once the content of a person's ego and contributed to maintaining ego cohesion, is left behind after their death. A prominent fraction of one's identity is inherited from the lineage one belongs to. The use of surnames is a way to let oneself be identified by people to which clan one belongs. This is not an identification from the outside, that having a family name enables, but the establishment of the self in the social scheme of ego interactions (interpersonal interactions). Having strong associations with one's clan may have an influence on the kind of archetypal channelization that the individual's libido goes through.

The desire to accumulate wealth comes from the ego's attempts to extend beyond the body. This desire to expand births the *Ego Economy*. Qualitatively, a human is not distinct from any other element in nature. It is to the credit of the ego, that one is able to differentiate between the 'self' and the 'other'. The personal ego acts as the string that holds the organism, preventing it from perishing. The fact that the ego does not extend beyond the body must have a cause, but it is not the impossibility of this occurrence that prevents it from spilling all over or nowhere at all. The spill that occurs during supposed spiritual experiences where people fail to distinguish themself from their surroundings, is a demonstration of ego malfunctions.

It is for the second time, I find myself lacking any available literature to supplement my ideas. At this point, I demand the reader to grant me permission to be auto-biographical to make advancements in the running theme. I believe a certain amount of liberty must be preserved to be autobiographical in matters like these, where there seems no apparent scope for any developments.

I have a red checkered shirt that I usually wear in winter. I was told that my grandfather had it stitched for himself in his youth. Later, my father wore it in his younger years, and now I do. My experience of wearing it is not an ordinary one. Possibly, the entire time I have it on my body, I subtly feel like a representative of my kin, especially when I wear it at the university. Placebo or not, the shirt is able to invoke memories of my family in me whenever I wear it. On days when I wear it, I am studying not as an individual but as a member of a lineage. Another experience, which is merely a piece of learned information at this point in time, dates back to my infancy. My mother tells me that at times, she would lend her chunni to the baby me while I slept. Assuming I am not going to end up as popular as Kakar, I think explaining the aesthetics of an Indian chunni to appeal to the Western palate is not required. My mother says that putting her chunni on her sleeping baby worked as effectively as marking her physical presence to him. Whether that be putting me to sleep, preventing me from crying, or keeping me engaged while she tended to the household chores, the chunni was as effective as it was tasked to be. As Winnicott would say, that mother lends her ego to the baby's developing ego, and her nurturance keeps the unthinkable anxiety at bay.[6] I propose to further develop this concept by adding the idea of *Ego Object,* an aspect of the self that can be extended from one person to another through the channel of objects.

I understand that the term "Ego Object" may give the reader the idea that this phenomenon of the ego exceeding the body is limited to tactile belongings that could be synonymous with "possessions." It is not just through the virtue of physical contact that objects come to be identified with the ego. As we learned earlier, the ego creates 'doubles' of itself in the form of shadow, reflection, and spirit. These *Ego Objects* are not merely identifications or passive components of the ego but are lively objects with an autonomy of themselves in some cases—mostly experienced only in fantasy or psychopathology. Let us revisit the myth of Narcissus once again at this point. I previously claimed that the reason why Narcissus was transfixed at the site of his reflection was not that he was in love with himself; instead, he was in love with his double, and it was to preserve the reflection that he chose not to make any movements. At this point with greater clarity on the concept of how the ego can indeed be traced outside the body, I intend to further develop the myth of Narcissus. In the moment the reflection came to be, Narcissus' body lost its ego to the reflection. In that moment the reflection was the real Narcissus, and it took command over his body. Narcissus could have chosen to preserve his life, which would have been the more intelligent way of exercising self-love, but it was not self-love that held him from leaving his spot. The only purpose his inaction served was to preserve the reflection—the *ego beyond the body.*

References

1. Piaget, J. (1929). *The child's conception of the world.* Harcourt, Brace & Company.

2. Fliess, R. (1953). *Ego and Body Ego* (p. 209). International Universities Press.

3. Ibid

4. Bhati, T. (2024, March 18). *Runanubandha - The skin's repository of yogic wisdom.* Yoga Cosmic Science. https://www.yogacosmicscience.com/2024/03/Runanubandha.html

5. Sadhguru. (2020). *Death; an inside story: A book for all those who shall die.* Penguin India.

6. Winnicott, D. W. (1965). *The maturational processes and the facilitating environment: Studies in the theory of emotional development.* International Universities Press.

Epilogue

As I set out to discover the multifaceted, dynamic nature of the ego, we explored its ability to dissolve itself, given the appropriate environment. Maintaining the same line of thought, we also discovered its libidinal economics and how it dries up without sufficient libidinal supply—just as a stream of water would without adequate flow. This libidinal arrangement is modulated by Will, which is the "driver" of the libido, much like the horse-rider metaphor that Freud gave in the context of the id-ego relationship. The ego is essentially an energy-demanding feature that occupies mental resources and requires a psychic environment to function. The body, affective states, identifications, and sensations are all part of the cluster that the ego sustains itself on. I set out to discover the nature of the ego, which I called the first-line features. Along the way, we ventured into a phenomenological view of the ego and how it organizes conscious experience, requiring conscious experiences to maintain what is called the "empirical ego." Borrowing phenomenological and psychoanalytic understandings, I applied them to the practice of meditation and studied the conscious ego in a rather unordinary setting. In psychology, the literature on the ego does not explore the possibility of its potential retirement. So, my findings are novel and open a scope for studying the organization of the human mind from a new perspective. I provided evidence for this retirement by tracing it in three functions of the mind, which are carried out by the conscious ego: time perception, communication, and containment of the unconscious. Through primary accounts and by referencing reputed literature, I substantiate my claim that "the conscious ego is indeed absent during meditation." The first chapter explores the dynamic feature of the ego—that it can morph itself and modulate its energy organization to facilitate the demands of other psychic functions.

The second chapter addresses the unconscious ego through its visceral aspects. We learn that the 'self' (as a synonym for 'ego') is influenced by the body it inhabits, in terms of bodily experiences and relationships with the environment and people around. Ego pathologies manifest their symptoms in the body, and the body, in return, can become a source of numerous pathologies. While all this is a basic psycho-somatic relationship, what really places the body ego as a legitimate contender to be seen as a sub-system of the ego is its role as the ground of genesis for mental functions like reality testing, affective regulation, and interpersonal relations. I followed the normative developmental model to formulate my ideas, though I understand that the shortcomings of self-permeance and other concepts related to the Eye Ego present an exclusionary understanding of human development, leaving no space for people with visual deficiencies. While my personal opinion is that people with visual deficiencies must rely on different sensations and experiences to ensure their existence, formally addressing this would have taken the work in a different direction.

The third and final section of the book, perhaps in itself, is the reason behind my decision to write a book. November of 2023 marked the beginning of a series of dissatisfactions in me regarding my dissertation supervisor and reader. My supervisor was quick to dismiss my idea that there could be something more to the script of the ego than the body. His arguments—backed by popular scientific "facts"—revolved around the essence of existence being survival and reproduction. I heard somewhere of a Buddhist teaching that says, "In moments of hunger, giving away your food will make you stronger." It is the truth in teachings like these, which go beyond popular science, that prevented me from deducing the essence of life to survival and copulation.

Each idea that I have formulated is in its nascent state, especially the Eye Ego, and they need further work to develop as legitimate systems in psychology. While not limiting myself to any one of these, I aimed to present a holistic and cross-disciplinary understanding of the ego, for which I referred to and abided by theories of the ego across various disciplines. Each sub-system and metaphor that I have proposed is a cotton strand in the fabric of the ego.

Appendix

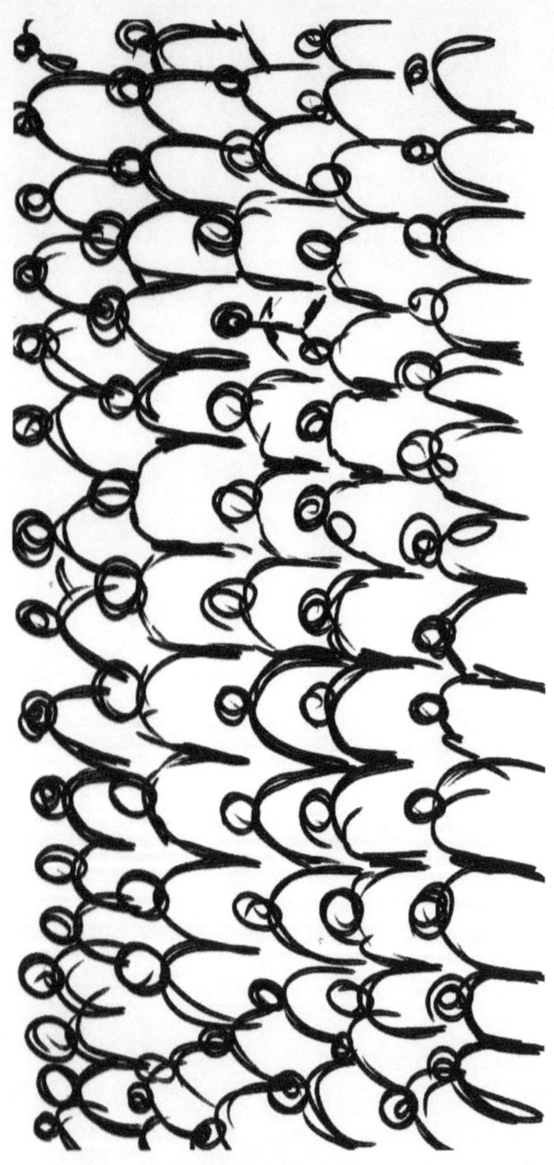

Ego Architecture

-    *"Sane" is what the majority is.*

The ego, as a psychic entity, emerges from the Id to manage conflicting aspects of the mind. While it originates in the Id, the ego is shaped by the demands individuals face throughout their lives, making it a co-creation of both internal and external realities. With the Id operating under the pleasure principle, the super-ego embodying parental morality, and the pressures of the world in play, the ego must constantly adapt and restructure the psyche to ensure the individual navigates these forces with minimal discomfort.

Classical psychoanalytic literature often presents the ego as designed to manage innate drives, primarily biological, that develop through a predetermined sequence of stages. However, later psychoanalysts, particularly in the Object-Relations school, acknowledged that the ego's development is also influenced by a nurturing environment and rich interpersonal experiences.

Note: I also reference these theoretical differences in the chapter titled Ego Nucleus.

These distinctions in ego development align with the ongoing Nature vs. Nurture debate. On one hand, some theorists argue that the ego unfolds according to a predetermined blueprint. On the other, some suggest that the ego is largely shaped by environmental factors. Personally, I've reflected on this subject enough to form my own perspective.

A significant portion of this text draws on bodily organs and their functions to support my ideas. In chapters like The Eye Ego, The Skin Ego, and Ego Nucleus, I explore the ego from a biological standpoint. Concepts such as the Eye Ego and Skin Ego represent the psychic manifestations of biological functions. In these cases, the body appears to be the only truth to which the psyche remains loyal. Here, the ego—or the psyche at large—adapts to its biological foundation. For example, I speculate that the act of 'seeing' plays a significant role in forming interpersonal relationships and ego dynamics. Similarly, the skin's sensitivity provides a canvas for the development and expression of the self. This biological perspective forms the dominant framework, which I assume reader is familiar with. After contemplating the ego's development for an extended period, I believe there's more to its story than is commonly understood.

The ego develops to mediate between the external and internal worlds, requiring a deep understanding of both. It evolves from the Id as a form of surface differentiation (as explained in The Ego and the Id) in response to external realities. Imagine the ego as a hardened layer forming on the surface of the Id. Drawing energy from the Id, the ego seeks to protect it from harm. Freud likens this relationship to a rider and a horse: although the rider is weaker, they direct the much stronger horse—not through force, but through skill. Similarly, as the ego becomes more familiar with the Id, it improves in directing its energies and using them efficiently. Just as a rider learns the temperament of their horse over time and becomes more adept at controlling it, the ego gains mastery over the Id by understanding its nature and functioning.

The ego, having developed from the Id, has an intimate knowledge of its workings, allowing it to negotiate with it effectively. However, the other entity the ego must contend with is reality itself. Rather than acting merely as an insulating layer between these different forces, the ego actively restructures the psyche, possessing its own form of intelligence. The intelligence I refer to here lies in the ego's ability to navigate these systems through its deep understanding of both realities.

While the ego understands the Id from the outset, its awareness of the external world is more distant and unfamiliar, requiring it to learn how reality functions. The ego can be compared to an algorithm that refines itself over time, accumulating information through experiences and exposure to the world.

Architecture of the ego

What I am suggesting is that the ego is a co-creation of the Id and the environment. While the Id is personal, the other force at play—the environment—is a 'given', and it becomes the individual's responsibility to adapt to it. What intrigues me is the fact that the environment is a shared space between members of a culture, implying that the ego, at least partially, is a collective construct.

The ego could never become a cohesively well-serving entity without knowledge of both the external and internal worlds. As a representative of rationality in the psyche, it seeks to bring 'order' to the inner world, the nature of which is socially determined. It is not an objective truth that the ego represents in its inner dialogue, but rather a reflection of popular reality. The ego is shaped by its interactions with the environment; the form it aims to attain is based on the prevailing model of sanity. What I mean by this is that there is an "optimal structure" for what an ego should be in any given environment. For example, there is a stark contrast between an urban male who engages in self-harm behaviors, like self-mutilation, and a boy from the Sambia tribe, who drains blood from his body as part of a rite of passage into manhood. While one person's self-harm may result from a fragment of the ego turning against itself, the

Sambian boy engages in the behavior to achieve his ego ideal. Just as in Foucault's idea that madness is a social construct (Foucault, M. (1961). Madness and Civilization: A History of Insanity in the Age of Reason (R. Howard, Trans.). Pantheon Books.), we learn that sanity, too, is a collective construct. A roadmap is laid down by the environment for the individual, and the ego develops in accordance with this popular model.

The story The Wise King by Khalil Gibran suggests a similar idea. In the ancient city of Wirani, there was a well that provided water to all its inhabitants. One day, a witch cast a curse on the well, proclaiming that anyone who drank from it would lose their sanity. The next morning, everyone in the city, except the wise king and his loyal chamberlain, drank from the well and went mad. As the day went on, the people noticed that the king and his chamberlain were behaving differently from everyone else. They concluded that it was the king and his chamberlain who had lost their minds. The citizens, united in their madness, demanded the king step down. Realizing that he could not rule a city where everyone thought he was mad, the king drank from the cursed well. His chamberlain followed suit, and with that, the king and his chamberlain shared in the madness of their people, restoring peace to the city of Wirani.

The ego does not adhere to a model of absolute reason, but rather to what is normative. Interpersonal relations are only possible when the participating egos share a basic script. There are popular folklore stories of children who, after being lost in the forest, were raised by a pack of wolves or monkeys. In these stories, the children often grow up walking on all fours instead of two. Unfit for human interaction, they are incapable of forming human relationships. As the ego develops in conjunction with reality, it internalizes the knowledge needed to navigate the external world effectively. A mother lending her ego to her baby's (Winnicott) has a profound impact on the child. The parental ego serves as a pathway for the development of the child's ego. It is not only the ego ideal—the standard the child aspires to—but also the current essence of the ego that is shaped by the parents' influence. I recall a remark I made in the chapter Ego Objects: parents often seek to mould their child into a 'double' of themselves, and one reason people have children is to extend their ego beyond their own body. This speculation complements the current argument. The child's ego, in search of a predefined path, begins with the parent's ego, and parents facilitate this process, offering the ego relief from the fear of destruction that accompanies the body's eventual death.

Cultural differences in people's psyche, such as their preference for independence or dependence on family, reliance on religion, and relation to their skin, can be traced through popular societal ideas. Social philosophies, art, and gender roles present themselves to the individual from the outside, and it becomes the individual's task to acclimate to them. The level of environmental adaptation an individual can achieve determines how cohesive their ego is. It is through this journey of adaptation to external reality that the ego forms its essence—just as it does through its connection with the id.

In 2017, an urban legend called चोटी काट spread across Delhi, where women reported that an unknown entity was mysteriously stealing their braids. The legend quickly gained traction, and many women came forward with personal accounts of their hair being taken. To protect themselves from this fear, people began hanging neem leaves at their doorways—a collective defense against a shared cultural threat. The thing that so many women reported these incidents was because—despite being irrational—they were not dismissed as "crazy" or "liars." Had the legend persisted for longer, with more women continuing to report similar experiences, it could have created a new 'reality' that other women's egos would need to accommodate—whose population would have shrunk by the day. However, the legend faded quickly, as it wasn't strong enough to take hold of the broader population's psyche. Yet, in a different social or historical context, the story could have been embraced within a relatively isolated community, where losing one's braid to an unseen force might have become a common belief–an accepted reality that the ego would have to adapt to. If such a belief becomes widespread, each woman would have to report having gone through such an incident. In that society, losing one's braid would be the order of the day. For an average woman, it would then become the responsibility of her ego to accommodate this popular reality by manufacturing a similar experience of losing one's braid–perhaps by repressing the memory of the woman cutting it herself.

An Archive

There exists a book authored by multiple people perhaps. सन्नोठ का इतिहास, along with some other things, it captures lineages of the families that have been inhabiting my village for the past centuries. It references a person named लाल मणि नौहवाल—the earliest known member of my family—who belonged to the 9th generation of my ancestors who lived here sometime during the 12th century CE. I can only imagine how the book's original author must have passed on his work to the next author with the intention that it gets nurtured and enhanced unbounded by the limitations of one lifetime.

I think I am growing out of that phase of my life where I would discard things that I could not comprehend, as "futile". Apart from this brief history account of my village, what makes me write this chapter is the first page of Sudhir Kakar's memoir: A Book of Memory, which states, "To my children's children, seeds yet unborn".

Intentionally or unintentionally, my family has always had dogs at all times; perhaps humans are not enough to exhaust my mother's nurturance. Except for one, Sami, all others were street dogs who, with time, occupied the small sitting places on the sides of my old house's Mughal arche-inspired entrance. This is my attempt to remember the dogs that my family has had relations with, and perhaps communicate about them to people yet to come.

You forget thing if there is nobody to tell them

~The Lunchbox

Tommy: A brown, weak Indie female dog who lived a full life of a little over 12 years. My mother tells me she was born in the winter a few months after my birth. Weak and tiny in stature, I remember her following me to my school bus at times. I never liked her name, "Tommy"; it was the name that every other dog was given in those days. It was my sister, along with some other kids, who named her one random day, of which I was informed later. Nearing death multiple times, she also suffered from eczema her entire life, and I remember her demise as my first realization of what death is.

Semi: An anxious female German Shepherd, born on December 3rd, 2014. She was brought from one of my father's friends after years of my persistent demand to have a pet. Our closed home turned out to be insufficient for her, and she had to be sent to an acquaintance.

Nanci: A small-sized black Indie female friend that Semi brought home with her, though Semi later grew jealous of her. Being a people-pleaser, Nanci would wag her tail while swaying her thick, blocky body—a trait she passed on to the next few generations: Hulk, Bulk, Bulki, Brownie, Choti, and Liza.

Sheru (the 1st) and Sheru (the 2nd) were both beautiful white male dogs whose reigns were contemporary to each other. I saw Sheru (the 1st) go through different stages of life, from being timid to becoming incredibly fearless in his last days, so much so that he would not be bothered even by a pack of hostile dogs. By the end of his life, his stature to me had become that of an elder human, whose presence commanded respect for the hardships and experiences he had endured. Sheru (the 2nd), also called Chota Sheru, never seemed to grow out of childhood. Found in the farmland by my father, he could be mistaken for a fur toy. With a long coat, even in adulthood, his face and innocence remained puppy-like.

Kalu: Named for his appearance, he was an abandoned dog whose growling made us aware of his presence in the tall grass near our under-construction house. It took him a few months to physically and emotionally recover from the beatings he must have received before being abandoned by his previous owner. Once recovered, it was not hard to guess why he had been abandoned. Gigantic in stature, he displaced both the Sherus with his hostile temper. Both he and the younger Sheru died of kidney failure within a few days of the initial symptoms appearing.

Shindy: A clever puppy, Shindy left his siblings and came to our house during the thick of last winter. Seeing him trying to please my mother one day, I said, "He has decided to live." None of his family members survived the winter. Small in stature, light brown in color, with a lean-muscular build, he has pointy ears like those of a German Shepherd. He has already had an elaborate medical history, though he is still under a year old. Now he lives with Oreo—another puppy who came a few months later—at our home. Well, "Oreo" is a name given to a dog to fit in with high society, but being humble, he prefers "Dhillu" and responds only when called by this name. Dhillu, a black-colored chunky puppy with white spots, is playful yet lazy. Though a little younger than Shindy, he already outweighs him by double. This new house has enough open space for them to play and run; their favorite spot to escape the heat this summer has been the madhukamini hedge. While writing this book, I have often heard fights break out between them, reminding me that dogs make the most painful sounds. They are still kids to me, and I hope they live full lives and depart as late as possible.

Male Etiquette

- *Male social etiquette is to tuck the phallus.*

It has been an observation of mine, that men—especially the young ones—make a significant shift in their tone and body posture while speaking with another man who is in power. This "power" may not just be in terms of social hierarchy but could be in terms of physical size, strength, or age. More prominent while speaking English, this shift is noticeable in Hindi in the choice of words. Their words become gender-neutral, and their body structure is a little shorter than usual. Even if two men with differences in their "power" do not communicate with language, the effect of the stronger's presence could be seen by the postural changes that occur in the "weaker" one's body. If the "weaker" man is in a seated position, he is likely to narrow the gap between his thighs in case another man is present nearby.

For a long time, I considered it a play of dominance and submission, but after one particular incident, it all just 'fits'. Cafes in Delhi often employ people to stand on the street to verbally advertise to people to come in. One such person—dressed as a clown—was asking people to come to a particular cafe in the most stereotypical gay voice. It appeared to me that under the garb of his tone, he was concealing his phallus—his phallus, which would have been unideal for attracting male customers. The mental imagery that left me was the Air India mascot welcoming the passengers in but with his phallus tucked between his legs. So submissive and un-hostile, as if not even a man.

Just as a young boy with the fear of being castrated by his father learns to appear submissive and phallus-less, men of all ages find ways to negotiate with other powerful men by appearing un-manly. To cope with the fear of castration, men perhaps self-castrate for a brief period to later turn up as more vital. This reminds me of Arjuna, who, during his incognito exile—*Agyat Vas,* with his brothers, turns into Brihannala, a female dance teacher.

A male child, often with no conscious objective, tucks his phallus between his thighs while being naked and cherishes the "V" shape that emerges. This perhaps makes him realize that his sex symbol could, in fact, be withdrawn from the world.

Acknowledgement

There is no one person in specific—counting out my socially isolated self—who is to be thanked.

In the process of reading for this and my academics in general, I am frequently taken over by feelings of gratitude in regard to web portals like *Anna's Archive* and *pdfdrive.com,* for letting me–and others of my kind–access to the world of knowledge which would have been alien otherwise. Some time ago, I heard on the web what having a bookshelf at one's home means. Having a bookshelf means one belongs to a family with a tradition of reading; in the lack of such an environment, PDFs came as a blessing to me.

If I were confident in the quality of my work and was sure that I wouldn't embarrass people by mentioning them in a disastrous piece of work, I would thank my parents for letting their adult son have his desired amount of time in his room and not trying to persuade him for anything. One thing I know for certain is that this book would not make any monetary gains for me, and I am grateful to them for letting me spend time being "unproductive".

I am grateful to thinkers like Sigmund Freud and Carl Jung for being so brilliant at their work. Reading Psychoanalysis brings intellectual satisfaction to me, and one of my aims has been to invoke in the reader something similar to what these people cause in me.

Reserving nothing for the next time, as there may never be a "next time" in case all five buyers of this book cyber-bully me for deciding to get such a pile of rubbish published, I would like to acknowledge my professors at Ambedkar University, for it was their listening to my yap that gave me enough confidence to write a book.

Notes

Notes

Notes

Notes